OREGON

OREGON BY ROAD

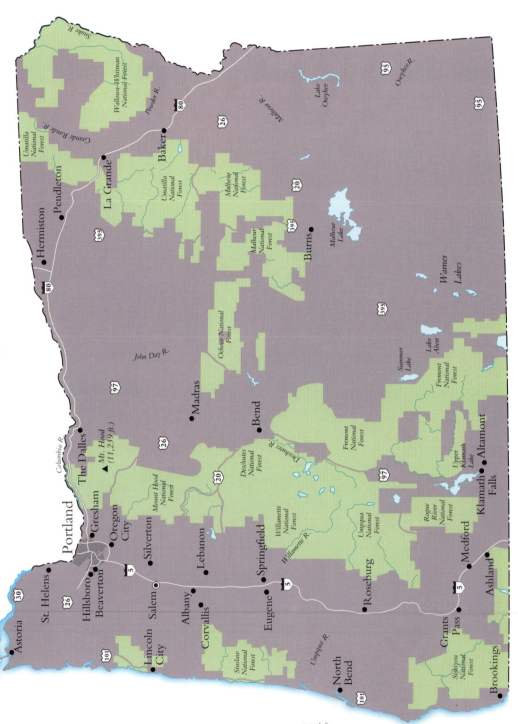

CELEBRATE THE STATES
OREGON

Rebecca Stefoff

BENCHMARK BOOKS

MARSHALL CAVENDISH
NEW YORK

Benchmark Books
Marshall Cavendish Corporation
99 White Plains Road
Tarrytown, New York 10591-9001

Library of Congress Cataloging-in-Publication Data
Stefoff, Rebecca
Oregon / Rebecca Stefoff.
p.   cm. — (Celebrate the states)
Includes bibliographical references and index.
Summary: Surveys the geography, history, people, and customs of one of
the three states that make up the region known as the Pacific Northwest.
ISBN 0-7614-0145-8 (lib. bdg.)
1. Oregon—Juvenile literature. [1. Oregon.] I. Title. II. Series.
F876.3.S735   1997   917.95—dc20   96-34984   CIP   AC

Maps and graphics supplied by Oxford Cartographers, Oxford, England

"Roll On, Columbia," words by Woody Guthrie, music based on "Goodnight, Irene" by Huddie Ledbetter
and John A. Lomax. TRO ©1936 (Renewed) 1957 (Renewed) and 1963 (Renewed) Ludlow Music, Inc.,
New York, New York. Used by permission.

Photo research by Ellen and Matthew Dudley

Cover Photo: *Photo Researchers, Inc.*, George Ranalli

Printed in Italy

1   3   5   6   4   2

CONTENTS

INTRODUCTION OREGON IS . . .   6

1 GEOGRAPHY   A BEAUTIFUL LANDSCAPE   10
VOLCANOES AND RIVERS • THE WET WEST • THE DRY EAST • OREGON WILD
AND TAMED • SONG: "ROLL ON, COLUMBIA"

2 HISTORY   YESTERDAY AND TODAY   32
THE WORLD APPROACHES • THE OREGON TRAIL • STATEHOOD • INTO THE
TWENTIETH CENTURY

3 GOVERNMENT AND ECONOMY   MAKING LAWS AND MONEY   52
INSIDE GOVERNMENT • A LEADER IN LAWMAKING • WORKING IN OREGON •
RECIPE: FROSTY FRUIT SMOOTHIE

4 PEOPLE   LIVING IN OREGON   70
ETHNIC OREGON • THE GOOD LIFE

5 ACHIEVEMENTS   AMAZING OREGONIANS   86
WRITERS • THE ARTS • POLITICS AND SCIENCE • SPORTS

6 LANDMARKS   OREGON ROAD TRIP   104
A CITY OF MANY NAMES • THE COAST • HEADING INLAND

STATE SURVEY   125
STATE IDENTIFICATIONS • SONG • GEOGRAPHY • TIMELINE • ECONOMY •
CALENDAR OF CELEBRATIONS • STATE STARS • TOUR THE STATE • FUN FACTS

FIND OUT MORE   140

INDEX   142

OREGON IS . . .

To the pioneers Oregon was a paradise.

"[Father] told us about the great Pacific Ocean, the Columbia River and beautiful Willamette Valley, the great forests and the snow-capped mountains. He then explained the hardships and dangers, the suffering and the dreary long days we would journey on and on before we would reach Oregon."

　　　—Martha Gay, who came to Oregon at age fourteen in 1851

"Here we are at last in Oregon City . . . that long looked for place!"

　　　—settler Esther Hanna, 1852

Today people still follow their dreams west.

"I wanted nothing more than to live in that most charmed of places . . . that Oregon."　　　—Sallie Tisdale, Oregon writer

"This place is more like the America that I grew up in. It's a little purer, a little simpler than other places."

　　　—a recent arrival from the East Coast

Oregon's history reaches far into the past . . .

"And before we know it, we are flying down the freeway, gazing out across this time-deep land where, as we sometimes forget, so much has happened."　　　—Terence O'Donnell, Oregon historian

"Today, Jacksonville's future lies in her past. Part of the business district looks much as it did at the turn of the century. The citizens of Jacksonville have preserved their past by restoring many historic buildings."

—Chamber of Commerce, Jacksonville,
National Historic Landmark District

. . . and its people are planning for the future.

"Sure I'm gonna rebuild. This place is my home!"

—Oregonian who lost his house in the flood of 1996

"More than half a million people are expected to move here by the year 2010. Let's be ready for them."

—Vera Katz, mayor of Portland, 1995

Oregon has a little of everything. Within its borders are mountains, gentle valleys, caves, old-growth forests, wild rivers, glorious beaches, and deserts. Native Americans, white and black Americans, and immigrants from Asia and Latin America meet and mingle here. Farms and orchards share the landscape with fast-growing cities and high-technology industries, but wilderness remains close at hand. Oregonians believe that everyone else secretly wants to be in Oregon. Maybe they're right.

1 A BEAUTIFUL LANDSCAPE

Mount Hood, Oregon's highest mountain peak

Oregon is one of the three Pacific Northwest states. The others are Washington and Idaho. Oregon lies on the West Coast of the United States, bordered on the west by the Pacific Ocean, on the south by California and Nevada, on the east by the Snake River and Idaho, and on the north by the Columbia River and Washington.

William Broughton of Great Britain spent three weeks on the Columbia River in 1792. Broughton, one of the first Europeans to explore Oregon and describe it for the rest of the world, called it "the most beautiful landscape that can be imagined."

Like many travelers after him, Broughton saw Oregon's lush forests, its meadows filled with flowers and berries, and its abundant wildlife. But this green and fertile garden was only the living surface of the land. Beneath it lay the bones of the earth, formed in fire and flood.

VOLCANOES AND RIVERS

For millions of years the eastern part of Oregon and Washington seethed and bubbled. From time to time lava burst from volcanoes or from huge cracks in the earth to flow like fiery mud over thousands of square miles of territory. The lava cooled and hardened into the high, flat plateau that is central and eastern Oregon.

Later, around 12 or 13 million years ago, the earth pushed up a

The Painted Hills of central Oregon, striped gray-green, gold, red, and pink, are made of ash that rained down during long-ago volcanic eruptions.

new range of volcanic mountains in western Oregon. Today these mountains are called the Cascades. Some of them are still active volcanoes. In Portland, Oregon's largest city, people sometimes see smoke or steam rising from the top of nearby Mount Hood.

Eight thousand years ago—just yesterday, in the earth's long history—one of the peaks in the southern Oregon Cascades blew its top. "That explosion must have been the loudest noise ever pro-

Crater Lake in southern Oregon, the deepest lake in the United States, formed after a volcano blew its top eight thousand years ago.

duced in this part of the world," says an Oregon volcanologist. Water filled the huge, empty crater and became Crater Lake, which is almost five miles wide and two thousand feet deep.

Even today the Pacific Northwest is frequently shaken by earthquakes, which often occur around volcanoes. In 1993 a quake rattled Portland and was felt for hundreds of miles, a reminder of the earth's awesome power. The center of the quake was thirty miles south of Portland. Earthquake expert Ian Madin warned Portlanders, "There's no particular reason to believe that the next one isn't going to be closer to home."

Water as well as fire has helped shape Oregon. The largest river in the state is the Columbia, which flows south from Canada and then turns west to the Pacific. Over many centuries this powerful river carved its channel through layer upon layer of rock, so that it now flows to the sea through the Columbia Gorge, a narrow passage between high, sheer cliffs. The north side of the gorge is Washington, and the south side is Oregon.

Hells Canyon is another river gorge, located on Oregon's eastern border with Idaho. Here the Snake River winds through a rugged canyon that is eight thousand feet deep in places—several thousand feet deeper than the Grand Canyon. After riding a raft through the white water of the Snake River, travel writer Richard Lovett called Hells Canyon "one of the least known but most spectacular places in North America."

Rivers have cut other, smaller canyons into Oregon's high central plateau. The Deschutes and John Day Rivers flow into the Columbia. In western Oregon the Rogue and the Umpqua race from the Cascades down to the sea.

The Willamette River also runs through western Oregon but it does not empty into the sea. Instead it flows north through a wide valley to meet the Columbia. Although most of Oregon's rivers are filled with rapids and waterfalls that make them difficult to navigate, the Willamette is broad and flat. The early settlers used it as a "highway" for travel in western Oregon.

Oneonta Gorge, where a creek flows into the Columbia River. In summer hikers walk up this narrow canyon, ankle-deep in the cool stream.

Sometimes, though, the rivers turn deadly. In February 1996, unusually warm temperatures melted snow in the mountains of western Oregon. Snowmelt poured downhill and mixed with heavy rains. Twenty-six rivers flooded. As the rivers kept rising, volunteers and National Guard crews worked around the clock to pile sandbags along Portland's Willamette River and in front of shops and homes in dozens of towns. A woman who skipped work to help a sandbag crew in Milwaukie said, "I got to the point of saying my community is more important than my job."

The floods left seven Oregonians dead, one missing, and forty-six injured. Nearly 22,000 people had to leave their homes. Most returned to mud-soaked floors and ruined furniture. "The things you lose . . . aren't your carpet or your sofa," a woman in the small town of Mist said sadly. "It's when you open up that cedar chest and there are the letters from your kids, destroyed by water and mud."

Most people picture the Pacific Northwest as a green place—a land of immense trees, mossy forests, and lots of rain. But that is only half of the picture. Oregon is divided by the towering spine of the Cascade Range, which runs north and south and cuts the state in two. People who live west of the Cascades are called wetsiders, while those who live to the east are drysiders.

THE WET WEST

The western third of Oregon is the land of trees, moss, and rain. The area between the Pacific Ocean and the Cascade Range gets between 20 and 130 inches of precipitation each year, with rainfall heaviest at the coast. In the mountains much of this

LAND AND WATER

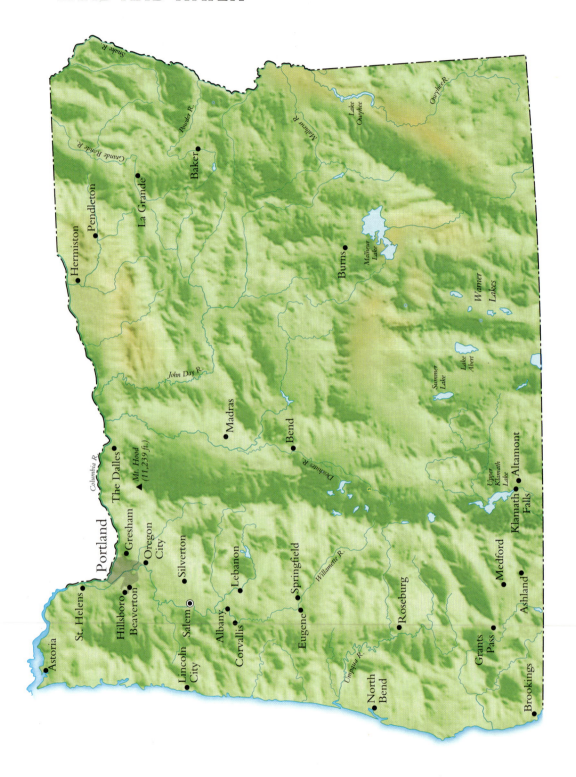

Snake R.

Powder R.

Grande Ronde R.

Baker

La Grande

Pendleton

Hermiston

Malheur R.

Lake Ouyhee

Ouyhee R.

Burns

Malheur Lake

Warner Lakes

Summer Lake

Lake Albert

John Day R.

Madras

Bend

Deschutes R.

Columbia R.

The Dalles

Mt. Hood (11,239 ft.)

Gresham

Oregon City

Portland

Silverton

Lebanon

Springfield

Upper Klamath Lake

Klamath Falls

Altamont

Medford

Ashland

Willamette R.

Roseburg

Hillsboro

Beaverton

St. Helens

Salem

Albany

Corvallis

Eugene

Grants Pass

Astoria

Lincoln City

Umpqua R.

North Bend

Brookings

"Oregon mist" can't keep this mother from hiking with her daughter on Mount Hood. The people of western Oregon have learned to live with rain.

precipitation falls as snow. Elsewhere it comes as rain—the soft, steady drizzle called Oregon mist.

Between October and May it can rain almost every day. The constant gray gloom gets on some people's nerves. A pioneer girl said, "My most vivid recollection of that first winter in Oregon is of the weeping skies and of Mother and me also weeping." Modern wetsiders have learned to live with the rain. "Like many Oregonians," says resident Catherine Windus, "I often shun raincoat and umbrella during heavy showers, preferring to pretend it's not happening."

On the good side, the steady rainfall nourishes western Oregon's

Ferns and mosses create a lush green carpet in western Oregon's forests. This old-growth forest has never been logged.

forests of huge cedar and fir trees and makes the region a fertile farming area. Western Oregon has a long growing season. Temperatures are generally mild. Along the Willamette, for example, winter temperatures very rarely reach the freezing point, and summers usually bring no more than a handful of 90-degree days.

Western Oregon is a geography sandwich: a valley between two mountain ranges. The Coast Range runs along the edge of the Pacific. The Coasts are low, rounded mountains, wrapped in fog and heavily forested with spruce, cedar, and fir. In southern Oregon the Coast Range merges with a knot of taller, craggier peaks: the Siskiyou and Klamath ranges, which sprawl across the Oregon-California border. Oregon writer Sallie Tisdale calls the Klamath and Siskiyou region "a bleak, lonesome, extraordinarily beautiful place—beautiful the way the moon is beautiful, or a comet come to earth, or the spatter of stones across a beach."

The center of western Oregon's "sandwich" is the Willamette Valley, flat and fertile in the north, hilly in the south as it begins to rise toward the mountains. East of the valley is another chain of

Broken Top, a jagged peak in the Oregon Cascades. Winter's carpet of snow brings skiers and snowboarders to recreation sites throughout the mountains.

mountains: the long line of the Cascades, separating west from east. At 11,235 feet, Mount Hood in this range is Oregon's highest peak. The central and southern Cascades are dotted with lava fields and lakes.

The western slopes of the Cascades receive plenty of moisture, carried inland from the sea. They are covered with tall forests of Douglas fir, hemlock, cedar, and spruce and are carpeted with mosses and ferns. But the high peaks keep rain-carrying clouds from traveling eastward, and the mountains' eastern slopes have drier, more open forests of ponderosa pine.

THE DRY EAST

The eastern two-thirds of Oregon is a high desert plateau with mountains around the edges. The plateau receives eleven to seventeen inches of rain and thirteen to eighty-five inches of snow each year. Summers are hotter than on the west side of the mountains, and winters are sunnier but colder. Temperatures as high as 119 degrees Fahrenheit and as low as −54 degrees have been recorded in eastern Oregon.

Much of this dry landscape is reddish brown rock, sparsely covered with silvery green juniper and wild sage shrubs. In the spring and summer, though, the plain blazes with wildflowers: purple-blue lupins, orange-red Indian paintbrush, and hot pink fireweed.

In the northeast corner of the state are the low but rugged Blue Mountains and the Wallowa Mountains near Hells Canyon. The Wallowas, with their snowcapped granite peaks and alpine meadows and lakes, are sometimes called Oregon's Switzerland.

Farms and ranches nestle among the rolling hills of central and eastern Oregon. The state's "dry side" has hot summers and cold winters.

Southeastern Oregon is part of the Great Basin, the vast arid region that covers most of Nevada and parts of Utah, California, and the Southwestern states. This part of Oregon is extremely dry. Its largest bodies of water are Harney and Malheur Lakes. In the wettest years Malheur Lake covers 125 square miles, but in dry years it shrinks until nothing is left but mud holes.

The southeastern corner of the state is a jumble of small ranges: the Mahogany, Trout Creek, Sheepshead, and Pueblo Mountains. The area's tallest peak, 9,670-foot Steens Mountain, rises sharply from the Alvord Desert, where tumbleweeds whirl across sands glistening white with salt. "Expect extreme hot, extreme cold, and oversized mosquitoes, but what country!" said Portlander Sandra Dorr after visiting Steens Mountain.

OREGON WILD AND TAMED

For centuries salmon have returned from the sea each year to lay their eggs in Oregon's rivers. Trout also live in the state's rivers and streams. Zane Grey, the famous author of many tales of Western adventure, was a fisherman who called the Rogue River "the best trout stream in the world." The rivers are also home to otters, beavers, and many kinds of waterbirds. Kingfishers, ospreys, ibises, sandhill cranes, blue herons, and eagles nest near Oregon's waterways or rest there during their yearly migrations.

Bears, wolves, and elk once roamed Oregon's forests. Wolves are thought to be extinct in Oregon now, and bears are seldom seen except in the wooded south. Mule deer and pronghorn antelope live east of the mountains. Cougars still prowl remote areas. At night the eastern canyons echo with the yipping of coyotes. These wild relatives of the dog appear as gray-brown shadows in fields and even in suburbs all over the state.

Oregon's most famous wild creature probably does not even exist. According to Native American legends and modern tales, the mountain forests are home to the Sasquatch, or Bigfoot, which

Salmon returning from the sea to lay their eggs in Oregon's streams fight their way upriver, leaping up waterfalls, rapids, and the spillways of dams.

The great blue heron nests along many of Oregon's waterways. Portlanders have adopted the stately heron as a symbol of their city.

WHOO'S FORESTS?

At a foot-and-a-half tall, with dark eyes and soft brown feathers dotted with white, the spotted owl doesn't look like a trouble-maker. But since the late 1980s the spotted owl has caused count-less arguments throughout the Pacific Northwest.

Spotted owls live in the Northwest's old-growth forests, areas that have never been logged. Each pair of owls needs a thousand acres or more of forest to survive. Spotted owls cannot live in clearcuts, sections of forest in which all trees are cut down, or in the young forests that begin growing after an area has been logged. The owls are vanishing as old-growth forests are cut for timber. Scientists believe that only a thousand or so pairs remain.

The spotted owl has become a symbol of the conflict over the Northwest's remaining ancient forests. Environmentalists claim that the forests must be preserved because they are the habitat of an endangered species protected by law. Timber-industry representa-tives and loggers claim the environmentalists are "tree-huggers" who are only using the owls as an excuse to ban logging in old-growth forests.

A wildlife specialist with the National Audubon Society has said, "Each is terribly important in its own right, both the owl and the forest. Time is running out to save both." Meanwhile, a forest worker in the timber town of Idanha drives a pickup truck with a bumper sticker that reads "Loggers Are an Endangered Species." Both sides have turned to the federal government for support. Law-makers must try to answer the question: How can we protect the owls and the forests and still continue to har-vest the trees we need?

resembles both a human and an ape. In 1971 a high-school music teacher named Rich Brown said that he saw a Bigfoot near The Dalles, a city on the Columbia River. Brown raised his rifle but, as he said, "I couldn't shoot it because it looked more human than animal." There is no proof, however, that the Sasquatch is real.

Sasquatches may be invisible, but humans have left their mark on the land. The Willamette Valley, with its mild climate and fertile soil, was the goal of the first white settlers. The valley remains Oregon's heartland, home to the majority of Oregonians. Today it is a row of cities strung along a ribbon of interstate highway. At the top of the row, where the Willamette River meets the Columbia, stands Portland, Oregon's largest city. A third of all Oregonians live in Portland or close to it.

Oregon's largest monuments to human activity are the four huge dams that span the Columbia River. The Bonneville Dam in the Columbia Gorge was completed in 1938. The Dalles Dam, the John Day Dam, and the McNary Dam followed through the 1960s.

These dams have changed the Northwest in many ways. They make it easier for barges to carry agricultural goods from Oregon's central plains to ports for shipping around the world. They provide water to irrigate the dry eastern fields. Most of all, they produce hydroelectric power. Electricity is cheap in the Northwest, which makes the region attractive to industries that use a lot of power, such as metalworking and papermaking. The dams have allowed power companies in the Pacific Northwest to sell excess electricity to Los Angeles and other cities.

At the same time, the dams have turned one of the most majestic wild rivers in the American West into a series of sludgy lakes. They

ROLL ON, COLUMBIA

A series of huge dams were built along the Columbia River in the late 1930s. Folksinger Woody Guthrie remembers the invitation in 1940 to "come up to the Columbia River to the Bonneville and Grand Coulee Dams . . . to walk up and down the rivers, and to see what I could find out to make up songs about. I made up twenty-six." This is one of the most beautiful.

Other great rivers add power to you,
Yakima, Snake, and the Klickitat, too,
Sandy, Willamette, and Hood River, too;
Roll on, Columbia, roll on!   *Chorus*

Tom Jefferson's vision would not let him rest,
An empire he saw in the Pacific Northwest.
Sent Lewis and Clark and they did the rest;
Roll on, Columbia, roll on!   *Chorus*

At Bonneville now there are ships in the locks,
The waters have risen and cleared all the rocks,
Shiploads of plenty will steam past the docks,
So, roll on, Columbia, roll on!   *Chorus*

And on up the river at Grand Coulee dam,
The mightiest thing ever built by a man,
To run to great factories for old Uncle Sam;
It's roll on, Columbia, roll on!   *Chorus*

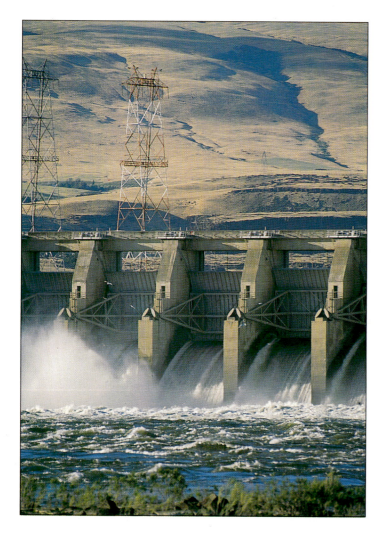

The Dalles Dam. The Columbia River dams had "a profound effect on all of the Northwest," according to Oregon historian Terence O'Donnell.

have created barriers to the migration of salmon, which have also been hurt by pollution and soil runoff from logging operations. Once salmon hatched in the Columbia in uncountable numbers. Today their population is dwindling fast.

Everywhere in Oregon people are changing the land. Ranchers graze thousands of head of cattle on the eastern grasslands, which are often owned by the federal government. Environmentalists point out that cattle pollute streams and destroy whole ecosystems, but ranchers believe that the land should be used to support families and communities.

A similar problem appears in fast-growing Portland. Developers want to cut down trees and build houses and malls on some of the parkland in which Portlanders take such pride. The struggle is sure to continue between those who want to protect what is left of wild Oregon and those who want to complete its taming.

2 YESTERDAY AND TODAY

Mount Hood *by Albert Bierstadt*

The first Oregonians were the ancestors of today's Native Americans. They came to Oregon ten thousand years ago, or perhaps a bit earlier. They settled first on the eastern and central plateau, and then along the Columbia, and finally on the coast.

Gradually they formed almost a hundred different bands and tribes. The Cayuse and other tribes of northeast Oregon had acquired horses from the Spanish by the eighteenth century. Mounted on horseback, they roved from the Wallowa Mountains to the highlands of Idaho and eastern Washington. Native Americans in southeastern Oregon coaxed a meager living from that barren land, eating roots and waterbirds and dwelling in huts of woven willow. The peoples of the Klamath lakes region also hunted waterbirds, but lived in domed lodges dug into the ground.

Native Americans were most numerous on the coast, along the western Columbia, and in the upper Willamette Valley. The Chinook lived along the Columbia, while the Coast Salish, the Coos, the Umpqua, and others inhabited the coast. These peoples hunted game and gathered berries in the forest and fed on salmon and shellfish from the sea. Their canoes were carved from cedar logs, and their houses were built of cedar planks.

A Nez Percé fishing camp near the Columbia River. Like other Native Americans of the Northwest, the Nez Percé dried and smoked salmon for year-round use.

THE WORLD APPROACHES

The name *Oregon* is probably an Indian word, but no one knows its source. By the 1760s people in Europe and America were using it as the name of a big river that was thought to flow through the West. Gradually the term *Oregon country* came to mean all of the Northwest, including what is now the province of British Columbia in Canada.

THE COYOTE GOD

Tommy Thompson was a chief of the Wy-am people along the Columbia River. Before he died in 1951 at the age of 108, Thompson passed on the Wy-am legends to younger members of the tribe.

Many legends tell of Spilyay, or Coyote. Spilyay was a wise, clever, mischievous god, sometimes called the Trickster. He played tricks on other animals and on people, but he helped them, too.

In the time before men and women lived on the earth, the salmon could not leave the ocean. Coyote was a giant, and very powerful. He dug a long, deep trench east from the ocean so that the salmon could swim upstream to have their young. That is how the Columbia River came to be.

Coyote is known as the Changer because his great trench changed the world. After the salmon could swim upstream, the earth was ready to be a home for men and women. The first people appeared in the world during this Changing Time.

Whites first came to Oregon looking for a waterway called the Northwest Passage. They hoped that the passage would be a trade route linking eastern North America with the Pacific Ocean. Explorers never found this Northwest Passage, because it does not exist. But they did explore Oregon, first by water and later by land.

Spanish and British sailors began exploring the Oregon coast in the sixteenth century. The first white American to set foot on the coast of Oregon was Robert Gray, a Boston sea captain, who landed there in 1788. Four years later, on another voyage, Gray came upon the Columbia River, which he named for his ship.

"Ocean in view! Oh! the joy!" wrote William Clark in his

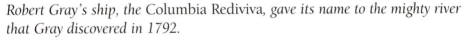

Robert Gray's ship, the Columbia Rediviva, *gave its name to the mighty river that Gray discovered in 1792.*

journal on November 7, 1805. No wonder Clark was overjoyed to see the Pacific. Together with his companions—Meriwether Lewis, forty or so other men, and a Shoshone woman named Sacajawea—Clark had been traveling toward the ocean for eighteen months, all the way from St. Louis, Missouri.

President Thomas Jefferson had sent army officers Lewis and Clark to find a route across North America. They traveled through the Louisiana Purchase, the vast territory between the Mississippi River and the Rocky Mountains. After buying the Louisiana Purchase from France in 1803, Jefferson sent Lewis and Clark to explore and map the new territory, which would eventually form the central United States. Jefferson also asked the explorers to find a route to the Pacific Ocean.

Lewis and Clark and their party were the first known Americans to cross the continent to its western coast—and back again. They returned from their journey with new information about the peoples, wildlife, climate, and geography of the Northwest.

Meriwether Lewis was particularly enthusiastic about the Willamette Valley. He called it "the only desirable situation for a settlement which I have seen on the West side of the Rocky Mountains." Lewis believed the valley could hold as many as 50,000 Americans. He would be amazed to see a million people living there now.

The Lewis and Clark expedition excited Americans about Oregon. But the Oregon country was not yet part of the United States. It was claimed by both the United States and Great Britain. In 1818 the two nations agreed to share the territory, opening the way for American settlement in Oregon.

Sacajawea, a Shoshone woman, was one of several guides and interpreters who helped Meriwether Lewis and William Clark make their journey to the Pacific Ocean.

THE OREGON TRAIL

Explorers, fur trappers and traders, missionaries, and settlers began trickling into the Willamette Valley in the 1820s. Many of them were helped by Dr. John McLoughlin, a Canadian official of Britain's great Hudson's Bay Company. McLoughlin was based in present-day Washington State, but because he was generous to the

American settlers in the Willamette Valley he is known today as the Father of Oregon.

In the 1840s the trickle of settlers became a flood. Thousands of people traveled westward on a wagon-train route that came to be called the Oregon Trail. The trail ran for 2,200 miles from Independence, Missouri, to Oregon City, just south of present-day Portland. A branch of the trail went south to California.

It was the lure of free land that drew the settlers west to Oregon. Between 1840 and 1870 a quarter of a million people crossed the continent on the Oregon Trail. Most of them traveled with their families, and many were children. Historian Lillian Schlissel calls their journey "one of the great migrations of modern times."

"We were a happy carefree lot of young people, and the dangers and hardships found no resting place on our shoulders," said Susan Parrish, who took the Oregon Trail at age seventeen. But the journey brought great hardship. Nearly every wagon train lost one or more people to disease, accident, starvation, or Indian attack.

The hardest part of the trip came at the end, in Oregon. The travelers were low on food and supplies. They had been on the road for months and were weary, and so were the oxen who pulled their battered wagons. But after the travelers dragged their wagons up one side of the steep Blue Mountains with ropes or chains, then lowered them slowly down the other side, they faced a difficult choice: Should they make the risky voyage by raft down the raging Columbia to the Willamette Valley, or should they try the brutal route across Mount Hood? "Today climbed a mountain that broke my animals' hearts. Near broke mine too," one pioneer who took the land route wrote in his journal.

"We did not know the dangers we were going through," wrote Martha Ann Morrison, who traveled the Oregon Trail at age thirteen. Despite the dangers, the wagon trains kept coming.

By mountain or river, settlers reached Oregon and began building communities. And as these communities grew, so did the feeling that Oregon ought to be part of the United States.

STATEHOOD

American settlers in Oregon begged the federal government in Washington, D.C., to take control of the Oregon country. One of

THE MOTHER OF OREGON

Tabitha Brown was sixty-six years old when she started out on the Oregon Trail in 1846. She wasn't looking for adventure. Brown joined the wagon train because two of her children were taking their families to Oregon and she did not want to be parted from them.

Brown's journey was not an easy one. A wagon overturned. A little girl died of scarlet fever, and a little boy fell under wagon wheels and was crushed. Then things got worse. In Idaho, Brown and a number of others from her wagon train decided to try a short-cut to the Willamette Valley. But their route led them into the Nevada desert and the Klamath wilderness. "Our sufferings from that time," Brown wrote later, "no tongue can tell."

Tabitha Brown was tough. Some of the travelers died, but she made it through to the Willamette Valley. She had lost everything but one small coin. Brown used that coin to buy needles and went to work making gloves. Eventually she made enough money to help build one of the oldest schools in the West, today known as Pacific University. The Oregon legislature named Tabitha Brown the Mother of Oregon in 1987.

War hero General Joseph Lane of Indiana, the first governor of the Oregon Territory. His arrival in 1849 brought the frontier territory under the rule of Washington, D.C.

them, a former fur trapper named Joe Meek, rode all the way to the nation's capital to make the request.

In 1846 the United States and Britain divided the Oregon country. Britain got the northern part, which is now British Columbia. Congress named the southern part the United States Oregon Territory and asked Abraham Lincoln to be its first governor. He turned down the job, so Congress sent General Joseph Lane instead.

By the 1850s the territory was growing fast. Asa Lovejoy and Francis Pettygrove founded a new town at the meeting place of the Columbia and the Willamette. They flipped a coin to see who would get to name the new town. Pettygrove won. He was from Maine, so he loyally named the town after the city of Portland, Maine.

Portland quickly became an important port and center of trade. Unlike some settlements in the Wild West, Portland was said to be orderly and respectable. An early historian of the city wrote, "Affairs of blood are not common; house breaking, violent robbery, or affrays are but few. Public tumult is unknown."

In 1853 the government made the northern half of Oregon into the Washington Territory. And on March 15, 1859, the ship *Brother Jonathan* sailed into Portland harbor with the news that Oregon had become the nation's thirty-third state. After being moved several times from its original location in Oregon City, the state capital was established in Salem.

Oregon's progress into statehood was not entirely peaceful. As early as 1847 George Abernethy, the settlers' elected leader, had warned of trouble with the Native Americans. "They see the white man occupying their lands, rapidly filling up the country, and they put in a claim for pay," Abernethy said. "They have been told that a chief would come out from the United States and trade with them for their lands; they have been told this so often that they begin to doubt the truth of it."

Trouble broke out that year in the Cayuse War, the first of a series of Indian wars in the Northwest. As the whites forced Indians off their traditional homelands, some Indians fought back. Wars broke out in the Rogue River area in the 1850s and in central and eastern Oregon in the 1860s and 1870s.

One man who became a symbol of the Native American struggle

The Cayuse War started when Native Americans killed missionaries Marcus and Narcissa Whitman and other whites near present-day Walla Walla, Washington. The Cayuse believed the Whitmans were spreading disease.

was In-mut-too-yah-lat-tat, born in the Wallowa Valley around 1840. His name means "Thunder Traveling to Loftier Mountain Heights." Whites knew him as Chief Joseph.

Chief Joseph became a leader of the Nez Percé people. In 1877, after gold was found in Nez Percé territory, the U.S. government ordered Joseph and his people to move to Idaho. After a fight in which three Nez Percé killed some settlers, Joseph tried to escape with his people to Canada. Men, women, and children traveled for 1,600 miles through the mountains into Montana, with the army in pursuit. At last, footsore, cold, and starving, the Nez Percé

Forced off their homelands, Nez Percé Chief Joseph and his people outfought, outwitted, and outran the U.S. Army for several months before surrendering.

surrendered. They were taken to Indian Territory in Oklahoma, where half of them fell sick and died. Chief Joseph ended his days on a reservation in Washington. He was never allowed to return to the Wallowa Valley.

INTO THE TWENTIETH CENTURY

Oregon's population and economy boomed after railroads reached the state in the 1880s. Portland grew fast, from 90,000 people in 1900 to 200,000 just ten years later.

Eastern Oregon's growth was based on gold, grass, and grain. Gold strikes lured prospectors to the state's interior in the 1860s, grass offered grazing for huge herds of cattle and sheep, and farmers in the northeast soon made wheat one of Oregon's leading exports.

Logging exports grew, too. By 1900 Oregon was the nation's third-largest producer of timber. Many of the fighter planes in World War I (1914 to 1918) were built of Oregon wood.

POPULATION GROWTH:

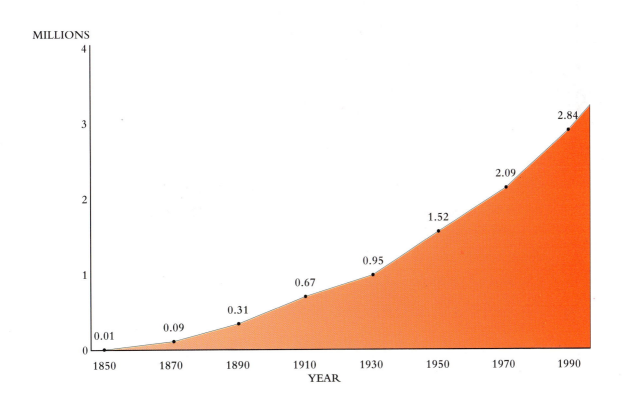

The Great Depression of the 1930s brought economic hardship to the entire United States, and Oregon was no exception. In 1934 Governor Julius Meier said, "Oregon is dead broke." Yet the Depression left a lasting legacy to Oregonians. The Civilian Conservation Corps (CCC) was a federal program to help the jobless by giving them work on public lands. In the state's national forests, CCC crews built roads, hiking trails, and bridges that are still used today.

The economic picture brightened when the United States entered World War II in 1941 and Oregon became a center of shipbuilding. War industries provided 160,000 jobs, attracting workers from other states. After the war, when soldiers returned to the United States and bought houses, America's timber industry boomed. Oregon became the nation's leading timber producer.

For decades Oregon was a well-kept secret. Oregonians were deeply attached to their state, but the rest of the country didn't pay much attention to it. The editors of *Oregon Times* magazine wrote that during the 1950s and 1960s "We existed largely as rumor, trudging along in a remote rainbelt and forever a little . . . out of it." But in 1975 a research organization announced that Portland was the most "livable" city in the country. Portland journalist David Sarasohn, only half joking, calls that announcement "the greatest natural disaster ever to strike Oregon."

Year after year the Pacific Northwest's reputation for "livability"

"You never saw such trees," wrote one amazed settler to the folks back in Missouri. A single tree could yield enough lumber for a house and a barn.

Oregon's forests have long provided the raw material for local industries. In the mid-twentieth century, for example, Portland became a center of shipbuilding.

grew. The populations of Portland and of Seattle, Washington, soared as people from other parts of the country moved to the Northwest. They loved the region's natural beauty, good schools, low prices and crime rate, and mild weather. Before long, old-time residents grumbled that the Northwest was becoming "trendy."

The rush of people to the Northwest has threatened the things that brought them here in the first place. Prices and crime have risen, and rapid population growth has put more pressure on the environment.

Oregon's population is expected to keep growing rapidly. Oregonians face the challenge of preserving what they love about their state for future generations to cherish. Science fiction writer Kate Wilhelm, who moved from Florida to Oregon, once said that Oregon's future is safe—as long as Oregonians continue to value their children and their trees.

3 MAKING LAWS AND MONEY

Oregon's state capitol in Salem

Even before Oregon was a U.S. territory, its settlers wanted to be governed by law. In 1843 a hundred settlers met on the Willamette River to form their own government. Dr. Robert Newell was one of them. He wrote, "After a few days' experience I became satisfied that I knew as little about the business of legislating as the majority of my colleagues."

Despite their lack of experience, the settlers managed to elect a sheriff and governor and to set up a government. They laid the foundation for lawmaking in Oregon.

INSIDE GOVERNMENT

Oregon's modern state government, like the settlers' government, was modeled on the federal government of the United States. The state government has three branches: executive, judicial, and legislative.

Executive. The executive branch of the Oregon government is responsible for carrying out every state function, from running the public schools to picking up litter along the highways. The executive branch includes six elected officials: governor, secretary of state, treasurer, attorney general, commissioner of labor and industries, and superintendent of public instruction. They oversee many agencies and thousands of employees.

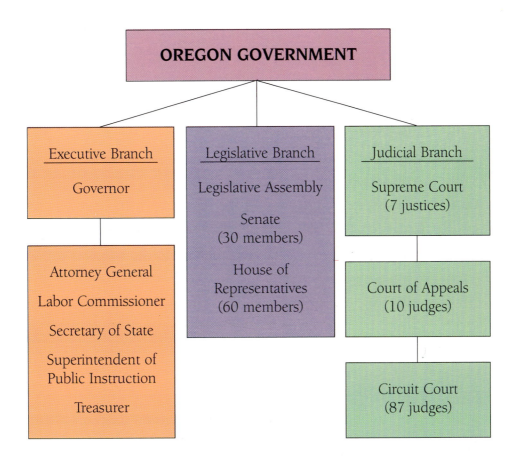

OREGON GOVERNMENT

Executive Branch

Governor

Attorney General

Labor Commissioner

Secretary of State

Superintendent of
Public Instruction

Treasurer

Legislative Branch

Legislative Assembly

Senate
(30 members)

House of
Representatives
(60 members)

Judicial Branch

Supreme Court
(7 justices)

Court of Appeals
(10 judges)

Circuit Court
(87 judges)

Judicial. Law cases are heard and decided in four different types of courts. Most trials, including criminal and juvenile trials, are heard in one of the state's twenty-two circuit courts, which have a total of ninety-two judges. Cases involving tax law are heard in a special Tax Court.

The Court of Appeals has ten judges. They rule on appeals, or challenges, to the decisions of the lower courts. The Oregon Supreme Court, with seven judges, is the state's highest court. All judges of Oregon courts are elected by voters to six-year terms. Cases involving federal laws are heard in federal courts.

Legislative. The legislative branch of the government is responsible for making laws, deciding how the state's money is to be spent, and debating public issues.

The Legislative Assembly meets in Salem, the state capital. It has two parts: a Senate and a House of Representatives. Oregon has thirty state senators, each elected for four years. It has sixty state representatives, who are elected for two-year terms. Oregon voters also send two senators and five representatives to the U.S. Congress in Washington, D.C.

In 1992 the people of Oregon voted to limit the amount of time officials could stay in public office. Officials' terms were limited to six to twelve years, depending upon the office. This controversial "term limits" measure was supposed to remove stuck-in-a-rut "career" politicians and make room for eager new public servants. The courts are still deciding, however, whether term limits are legal.

A LEADER IN LAWMAKING

Oregon has a history of making progressive laws that reform injustices or are ahead of their time. Between 1902 and 1908 Oregon passed a series of laws to make elections and lawmaking more democratic. Soon other states adopted "the Oregon system."

Elections were reformed by the direct primary, which allowed Oregonians to vote for candidates in the primary elections, in which party members choose their party's candidate for the general election. Earlier, people had voted for the party of their

Riders in the "Salmonmobile" urge voters to support a ballot initiative aimed at cleaning streams that have been polluted by livestock.

choice, and party officials had selected the candidates. Another reform gave voters the right to recall public officials, or remove them from office.

The most important reforms, however, were the initiative and the referendum. The initiative is a way for ordinary citizens to make new laws or changes to the state constitution. These new ideas, or initiatives, are included on the ballots of state elections. If the voters approve them, they go to the state legislature for action. The referendum lets any citizen ask the people of Oregon to vote for or against an action by the state government.

People who want to put their initiatives and referendums on the ballot must first collect a certain number of signatures from voters. In election years a lot of people earn money as signature gatherers. Groups that support initiatives pay the gatherers fifty cents or a dollar for every signature they collect. But some Oregonians are tired of hearing, "Will you sign my petition?" four or five times a day. "These petition people are a real nuisance," complained Sue Fleming while she shopped in downtown Portland. "I've had to brush them away like flies."

Oregonians have voted on initiatives dealing with the environment, with pay and benefits for state employees such as teachers, and with many other issues. One important initiative was Measure 5, which appeared on the 1990 ballot. Measure 5 set a limit on property taxes. It pleased people who worried that taxes on real estate were becoming too high, but it cut the amount of money available for schools and other government services.

Many public services have been cut back since Measure 5 passed. For example, public schools have had to cut some sports and arts programs. When universities began receiving less money from the state, they raised tuition. Some of Oregon's state parks may close. Libraries have shortened their hours and dropped some programs. One unhappy librarian said, "Sure, Measure 5 saved property-owners a few dollars today, but what are we doing to our future?"

No one is sure what the long-term effects of Measure 5 will be. But as a landowner who voted for the measure said, "Hey, the state listened to what the people want. That's democracy in action."

WORKING IN OREGON

The 1980s brought an economic boom to Oregon. The state's economy grew faster than the overall U.S. economy. Starting in

A WINGDING IN SALEM

Summer is state fair time in the capital city of Salem. People from around the state gather on the fairgrounds for a wide variety of events. A day at the fair can include South American music, sheep and cattle shows, a Spam recipe contest, Japanese sumo wrestling, a laser light show, and performances by entertainers like Bill Cosby.

Kids can become stars of the fair. In 1995 twelve-year-old Sterling Holmes won a cooking contest with his recipe for corn nachos. His prize was a mountain bike and a helmet. That same year fifteen-year-old Robin Marsh won two blue ribbons for her brown-and-white guernsey cows.

More that two thousand people work at the twelve-day fair. Attendance has dropped a bit in recent years, but the state fair is still a lively Oregon tradition.

EARNING A LIVING

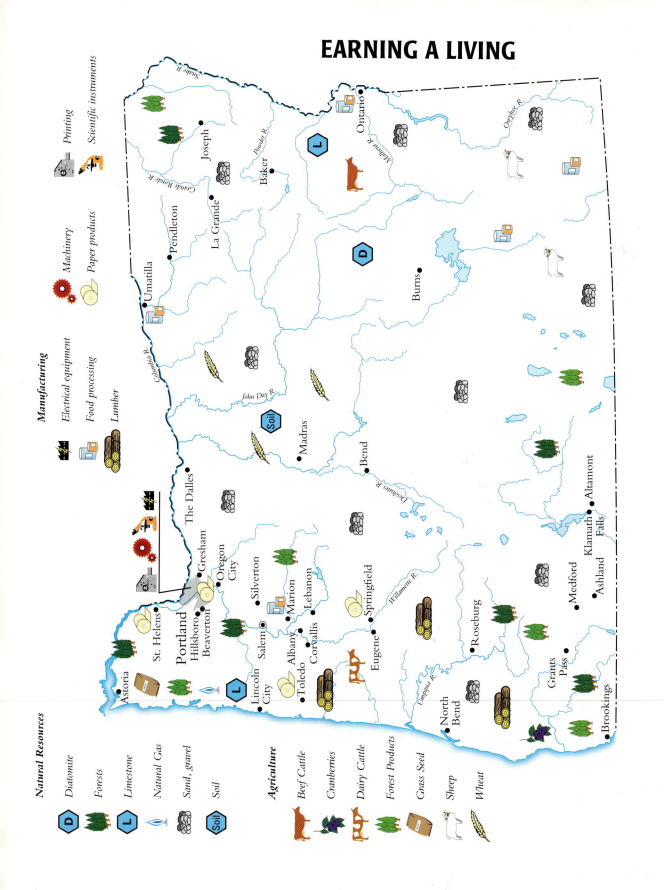

Printing

Scientific instruments

Machinery

Paper products

Manufacturing

Electrical equipment

Food processing

Lumber

Natural Resources

Diatomite

Forests

Limestone

Natural Gas

Sand, gravel

Soil

Agriculture

Beef Cattle

Cranberries

Dairy Cattle

Forest Products

Grass Seed

Sheep

Wheat

Snake R.

Joseph

Baker

Powder R.

Ontario

Malheur R.

Owyhee R.

Grande Ronde R.

Pendleton

La Grande

Umatilla

Columbia R.

John Day R.

Madras

Bend

Deschutes R.

Burns

The Dalles

Gresham

Oregon City

Silverton

Marion

Lebanon

Springfield

Willamette R.

Medford

Klamath Falls

Altamont

Ashland

Portland

Hillsboro

Beaverton

St. Helens

Astoria

Salem

Albany

Corvallis

Toledo

Eugene

Roseburg

Grants Pass

Lincoln City

North Bend

Umpqua R.

Brookings

1991, however, layoffs and the arrival of new workers produced a job shortage. By 1994 Oregon's jobs and income were still growing faster than the national average, but more than 7 percent of workers were unemployed.

Oregon's economy has always been based on resources from the land, rather than on manufacturing. Slowly, however, the economy is becoming more diversified. Jobs that provide services, especially services for tourists, are a fast-growing part of the economy. High-technology electronics and computer industries are on the rise. Oregon's Nike Corporation, which sells athletic shoes and clothing, is a business giant around the world. Forestry is still the leading industry, however, followed by agriculture and tourism.

Forest Products. Forestry has dominated Oregon's economy throughout the twentieth century. The timber industry cuts trees, ships logs, and turns them into boards, chips, cardboard, or paper at mills.

1992 GROSS STATE PRODUCT: $62.7 BILLION

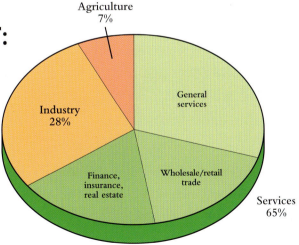

Agriculture 7%

Industry 28%

General services

Finance, insurance, real estate

Wholesale/retail trade

Services 65%

The timber industry has had problems in recent years. Workers blame environmentalists for cutbacks in logging and the loss of timber jobs. It is true that laws that protect some forest areas have hurt logging, yet there are other reasons why jobs are vanishing from timber towns throughout Oregon.

Take Reedsport, a coastal community of about five thousand people. In early 1996 the International Paper Company (IP) closed its nearby mill and sold its holdings in Pacific Northwest forests, wiping out 330 jobs. IP said that it closed the mill because the company already had more finished products on hand than it was selling. In addition, IP could make its products more cheaply in the South than in the Northwest.

Reedsport was hit hard. The town's major source of employment was gone. "A lot of people are looking for the mill to start," said Mayor Ted Walters. "But there are a lot of people also saying, 'I'm out of here.'" Carol Harris, a local bartender, feared that a permanent shutdown of the mill "would make a ghost town out of this place."

Some people who have worked at the mill all their lives are turning in new directions. "I consider my future down at IP, so I have to start over again at thirty-eight," said Mark Bedard, who plans to study business administration at a community college. He will receive financial aid from a federal job-training program for displaced workers. Felicia Bitek, a mill worker who wants to become an electrician, also applied for the program. "Going down there and getting tested after twenty years out of high school, I was very nervous," she said. She signed up for classes in math, computers, and blueprint reading.

Logs await processing at a mill, where they will be sliced into lumber or mashed into paper pulp.

Huge rafts, or islands of logs, are stored and moved on Oregon's rivers.

The timber industry faces an uncertain future. Timber workers, and whole timber towns, are trying to do what Felicia Bitek did. Many realize that to survive, they will have to change.

Agriculture. Agriculture is Oregon's second-largest industry. The state produces wheat, of course, but it is also the nation's top producer of some more unusual crops, such as Christmas trees, grass seed, hazelnuts, peppermint, and raspberries and black-berries. Farms and orchards yield large crops of strawberries, onions, cauliflower, prunes, apples, pears, and nursery and green-house plants.

Oregon's first cargo of wheat was shipped to Liverpool, England, in 1869. Today wheat remains one of the state's leading exports.

FROSTY FRUIT SMOOTHIE

What's a Marionberry? It's a cross between a raspberry and a blackberry, and it grows only in Oregon. One of the best ways to enjoy this sweet-tart berry is in a *frosty fruit smoothie*. Don't worry if you can't find marionberries at your grocery store; just use raspberries or blackberries—or both—instead.

1. Peel two bananas, wrap them in plastic wrap, and put them in the freezer. Also wrap and freeze 1 cup of fresh berries. (Or buy ones that are already frozen.) Leave the bananas and berries in the freezer for 24 hours.

2. Pour 1 cup of apple juice into a blender. Add the bananas. Blend at high speed. Now add the berries and blend again until the mixture is smooth. It should be as thick as a milkshake. If it's too thick, add a little more juice. Makes two servings.

Kids take part in a family cattle drive near John Day, in central Oregon.

Ships carry Oregon's agricultural exports around the world. South Korea, Japan, the Philippines, Pakistan, Saudi Arabia, and other countries buy its french fries, wheat, and grass seed.

The cattle industry contributes several hundred million dollars each year to the state's economy. Dairy farming and hay making are also big business, especially in western Oregon. The Tillamook

Valley, a low-lying plain covered with lush green grass, is a dairy cow's paradise and the center of the state's cheese industry. When the valley turned into a vast lake during the floods of 1996, farmers and volunteers worked desperately to save the cows. Still, many farmers lost their livestock.

Tourism. Tourism is a big industry in Oregon. It includes restaurants, hotels and motels, museums, recreational businesses, transportation, and more. The Pacific Northwest has become a popular vacation spot, and Oregon's economy is relying more and more on tourist dollars. By the middle of the 1990s tourism was bringing $3 billion a year to Oregon. The state's tourism office has nine welcome centers throughout the state to help visitors make the most of their vacations.

Why do people come to Oregon? "This place has everything!" said Jeff Margulies, a fourteen-year-old from New York, during his first visit to the state. "You can go snowboarding on Mount Hood in the middle of summer, and the same day you can go whitewater rafting. Plus it's real clean here."

Minerals and Energy. Gold is still mined in central and eastern Oregon and in the southern mountains. Some miners work their claims alone, like the old-time prospectors. Other mines are run by multimillion-dollar corporations. Environmentalists have raised concerns about pollution caused by these large operations, some of which use poisonous chemicals to treat the gold ore.

With both beaches and rocky mountains, Oregon is a good source of sand, gravel, and stone for road making and building. These materials are used locally and also exported to other states and nations.

"Awesome!" exclaimed one windsurfer after a day on the Columbia River. Wind rushing up the Columbia Gorge creates a paradise for windsurfers from around the world.

Oregon's natural-gas reserves will provide energy for the future. But the state also makes better use of renewable resources than any other state. One-quarter of all energy used in Oregon comes from hydroelectric power or from burning wood. Many people use solar or wind energy in their homes, and businesses are beginning to use these renewable, pollution-free resources as well.

Turbine generators in Umatilla harness the electricity produced by dams on the Columbia. Oregon's hydroelectric bounty lets it sell power to California and other states.

4 LIVING IN OREGON

Oregon has been called a "white" state. A 1993 study showed that there were slightly more than 3 million people in Oregon, and 90 percent of them were white. The population included 147,000 Hispanic Americans, 86,000 Asian Americans, 51,000 African Americans, and 45,500 Native Americans. Yet Oregon's population is changing and becoming more diverse. Twelve out of every hundred students in Oregon's public schools and universities are people of color.

ETHNIC OREGON

White people were a minority in early Oregon. In 1850 there were about 12,000 people in Oregon, but only 800 whites and 54 blacks. Most of the rest were Native Americans. A few Chinese immigrants had come north from California to work in the gold-fields of southern Oregon.

People of Scandinavian, English, Irish, Scottish, German, Polish, and Italian ancestry came to Oregon in large numbers in the late nineteenth and early twentieth centuries. Swiss immigrants started the cheese industry in Tillamook. Finns settled at Astoria and elsewhere on the coast and helped establish the fishing industry.

Many Chinese immigrants came to Oregon in the 1870s and 1880s to work building the railroads. After 1882, however, U.S.

Russian immigrants are among the most recent ethnic groups to have found a new home in Oregon.

laws prevented Chinese people from coming to the United States, and Oregon's Chinese population stopped growing.

Some old histories record that the first Japanese immigrant to Oregon arrived in 1860 and worked lighting gas lamps in Portland. A large number of Japanese men and women arrived in the 1880s to work on the railroads. Many of them stayed and became

Japanese immigrants and their Japanese-American children helped turn the Hood River Valley near Mount Hood into one of the finest fruit-growing regions in the United States.

successful fruit growers in the Hood River Valley near Mount Hood.

Like Japanese Americans all over the western United States, Oregon's people of Japanese ancestry were forced into special camps by the army during World War II, when the United States went to war with Japan. Many lost their houses and land. Afterward some Japanese decided not to return to their homes. Others came back, however, and reestablished the state's Japanese-American community. Linda Tamura, a Japanese-American writer who grew up in Oregon, praises the strength of the men and women from Japan who survived "racial persecution, language barriers, strenuous labor, and financial hardships, while still maintaining their dignity and a loyalty for their new homeland."

New Arrivals. African Americans had been coming to Oregon from the early days of exploration—one of the men who came west with Lewis and Clark was black. But Oregon did not have a large black population until World War II, when African-American workers were drawn to jobs in the state's war industries.

The most recent wave of Asian immigrants came to America to escape the Vietnam War and other wars in Southeast Asia. Between 1975 and 1993, 24,000 men, women, and children from Vietnam, Cambodia, and Laos settled in Oregon. They are working to forget old ethnic rivalries and to help one another. Says Paul Kinh Duong, "We quickly realized that we need to be together and support each other."

Many Southeast Asians have opened small restaurants or groceries in Portland. "Anybody work hard, they can succeed," says Pham Thu Trong, from Vietnam, who owns a small beef-noodle-soup restaurant. But life in America has brought new challenges. One new peril is the rise of Asian-American youth gangs that prey on other Asians. Because of the gangs, jeweler Nguyen Truc keeps steel bars over the window of his store. "Even in Vietnam, in wartime, we didn't have to do this," he says. "There might be too much freedom here."

For years Mexican and Latin American workers have come to Oregon each year to pick fruit and work on tree farms. Now many of them are staying. Hispanics are the largest minority group in

AN AFRICAN-AMERICAN HEROINE

One of the most distinguished members of Portland's early black community was Beatrice Morrow Cannady, who was born in Texas in 1889. She went to the University of Chicago before moving to Portland. In 1912 Cannady became an editor for the *Advocate*, Portland's African-American newspaper. One of the first women to practice law in the Pacific Northwest, Beatrice Morrow Cannady did everything she could to improve relations between blacks and whites and to help African-American artists.

The ancient Japanese art of taiko drumming enlivens a Buddhist festival in Portland. Taiko performers dance and play drums of different sizes.

Oregon, followed by Asian Americans, African Americans, and Native Americans.

"There's more competition than I thought here, but you can still get good work," said Fermin Carillo of Mexico after moving to Gresham, just east of Portland. Heriberto Aguilar moved with his wife and children from Mexico City to Canby. At first it was hard for Aguilar to communicate in English. Now he makes time each week to work with young Hispanic men and women, helping them to feel at home in the United States.

About one-third of Oregonians are regular churchgoers. The church with the most members statewide is the Roman Catholic

ETHNIC OREGON

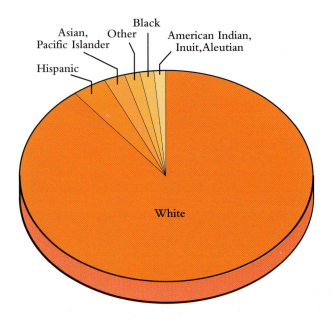

Hispanic

Asian, Pacific Islander

Other

Black

American Indian, Inuit, Aleutian

White

Church, followed by the Church of Jesus Christ of Latter-day Saints (the Mormons). Oregon has many different Protestant churches, and there are Jewish synagogues and Buddhist temples in the largest communities.

Fighting Racism. Not everyone welcomes Oregon's growing diversity. A few young people called skinheads (because they shave their heads) have insulted or attacked people of color. African Americans and members of other minority groups have had to battle prejudice and hate crimes.

One hate crime in early 1996 attracted national attention. Two white students at Oregon State University in the small town of Corvallis were convicted of harassing a black student. Led by students, two thousand people came together to speak out against racism. The rally was one of the biggest meetings in the town's history.

Kids at Wilsonville High School took action when racist graffiti started showing up on school walls. Fifteen-year-old Sarah Leitch passed out buttons with a simple but important message: "Respect." Students also planned to put up a "Hate-Free Zone" banner. Sophomore Adam Wolff said, "Like Martin Luther King says, you have to change people's habits first before you change their hearts."

THE GOOD LIFE

Oregonians believe that their state offers them a good life, and they want to keep it that way. They want good education and health care for all the people of the state, now and in the future.

CELEBRATING DIVERSITY

Ethnic groups share their heritage with other Oregonians in festivals large and small. On May 5, Mexico's national holiday, Portland celebrates with the Cinco de Mayo festival. Visitors munch on burritos and tacos, buy pottery and other Mexican handicrafts, and enjoy Mexico's magnificent folk dancers and singers.

Native Americans honor the traditions of the West at the Tygh Valley All-Indian Rodeo, held in The Dalles. German Americans and others enjoy the traditional German fall festival Oktoberfest in Mount Angel and the Sauerkraut Festival in Saint Helen's, where people enter cooking contests with their recipes for bread, cake, and even ice cream made with sauerkraut!

A rally against racism drew one of the largest crowds in the history of Corvallis, home of Oregon State University.

In 1991 the state legislature passed the Oregon Educational Act for the Twenty-First Century. The act required school districts to raise their academic standards, to get parents more involved in their children's education, and to prepare kids for community life. The act had high goals, but with the budget cuts caused by Measure 5, schools are finding it hard to put those goals into practice.

Oregon has a number of fine universities. The University of Oregon in Eugene is a center for higher education in law and business, as well as in liberal arts such as history. Portland State University in Portland is the state's only urban campus. It offers strong programs in education, engineering, and environmental studies. Oregon State University in Corvallis is known for its courses in forestry, agricultural science, and veterinary science. And Oregon Health Sciences University in Portland—on top of a hill called Pill Hill—is the state's only medical school and its seventh-largest employer.

Health care is important to all Americans. Oregon is a leader in health-care reform, as it was in legislation. Other states are considering reforming their health-care systems on the "Oregon model." Through the Oregon Health Plan, the state provides health care for unemployed Oregonians or those with low incomes.

For many Oregonians, the good life is the outdoor life. "I'm not happy unless I'm on my board," says seventeen-year-old Curt Evans. He's talking about windsurfing—standing on a surfboard that has a small sail and zipping across the choppy waters of the Columbia. Hood River Gorge on the Columbia is one of the best places in the world for windsurfing. On good days the brightly colored sails of hundreds of boards dance across the blue water like a swarm of butterflies.

Oregon has fourteen national forests that contain thirty-four wilderness areas. "What I love about my life here is that I'm never more than an hour or so from some kind of wilderness. Walking those trails, seeing the trees and the distant mountains, is the best exercise for your body and your spirit," says an Oregon-born woman who lives in Portland and hikes every weekend. A lot of people must agree with her. According to a survey in the early

A couple enjoys a quiet night of camping on a lakeshore at Mount McLaughlin.

1990s, Oregonians hike, camp, and ski more than most other Americans.

Settlers first came to Oregon to farm the fertile Willamette Valley. Today more Oregonians live in the Willamette Valley than on the coast, in the mountains, or in eastern Oregon. But these days many more Oregonians live in cities or towns than on farms. Portland and its outlying communities are growing fast. Salem and Eugene, both in the Willamette Valley, are major cities. Salem is the state's center of government, and Eugene is an important educational center. Other important cities include Newport on the coast, Medford and Klamath Falls in the south, and Bend, Pendleton, and The Dalles in the east.

TEN LARGEST CITIES

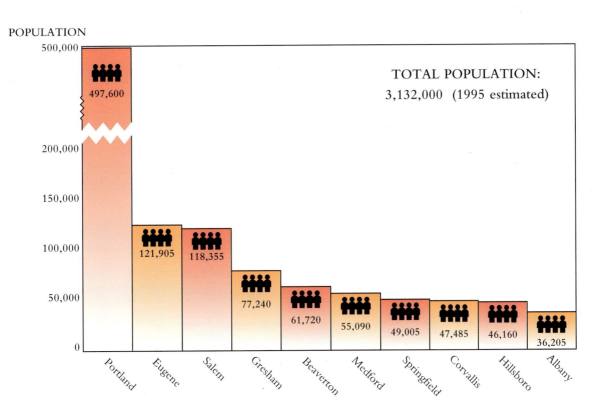

POPULATION

TOTAL POPULATION:
3,132,000 (1995 estimated)

Portland 497,600
Eugene 121,905
Salem 118,355
Gresham 77,240
Beaverton 61,720
Medford 55,090
Springfield 49,005
Corvallis 47,485
Hillsboro 46,160
Albany 36,205

Only Native Americans are permitted to take salmon from certain stretches of Oregon rivers.

Oregon's first residents have become city dwellers. Only one-tenth of the state's Native Americans live in the countryside, either on or off the nine Indian reservations. The largest of these reservations is Warm Springs, just east of the Cascade Range, where Native Americans operate a resort and casino that draw crowds of visitors from Portland and Washington State. The other nine-tenths of Oregon's Indians live in cities or towns.

Small-town life is still a big part of Oregon culture, however. "Portland's okay, I guess, but here I know all my neighbors," said a resident of tiny Troutdale, a town near the Columbia Gorge. A couple who left good jobs in Portland to open a store in much smaller Prineville explained, "A smaller town is a good place for our kids. They'll be close to nature, and they'll have fewer chances to get into trouble."

Some small towns are growing a bit as people leave Portland and out-of-state cities for a slower, more relaxed way of life. "One of the things I love best of all is no phones," says Patty Baca, who lives in Granite, population twelve. Granite is one of many ghost towns in the Wallowa Mountains, left behind when the local gold rush ended years ago. "Granite is not so much of a ghost town anymore," Baca says. "A lot of people are moving in and building. I think we've got three or four new people a year. It's a boomtown."

"A quiet country store beats a mall any time," says Anton Wiseman, who moved with his family from Chicago to a small town in rural Oregon.

5 AMAZING OREGONIANS

The Oregon Trail Pageant

Oregon has not yet produced a U.S. president, but it has produced a lot of talented people. These Oregonians are known far beyond their state's borders.

WRITERS

Oregonians like books. According to the *Oregonian*, the state's leading newspaper, Portland is "the Number 2 reading-est town in the country, after Seattle." Some people come to Portland just to browse the city's many large bookstores.

Maybe the people of Oregon read so much because the state is home to so many fine writers. One of them is Ursula K. LeGuin, the author of many award-winning books of science fiction and fantasy.

LeGuin fell in love with fantasy when she was a child. She read fairy tales and listened to her father, a well-known scholar of Native American culture, tell Indian legends. She began writing her own stories at the age of nine. Something important happened when she was twelve. She read a book of new fantasy stories and realized that "people were still making up myths." She says, "I had discovered my native country."

The Left Hand of Darkness is one of LeGuin's best-known science fiction novels. It is both a great adventure story and a plea to

Ursula K. LeGuin, one of the state's most respected novelists, has written tales of adventure on other planets as well as stories set in Portland and on the Oregon coast.

people to accept one another's differences with love and understanding. Another book, The *Lathe of Heaven*, is set in Portand. It is the story of a man whose dreams really do come true and a doctor who uses the dreamer to change the world.

LeGuin has written books for young readers, although they are enjoyed by people of all ages. The fantasy novels *The Wizard of Earthsea, The Tombs of Atuan,* and *The Farthest Shore* are about a boy who becomes a magician and joins the great battle between good and evil. *The Farthest Shore* won the National Book Award for children's literature.

Many of LeGuin's books are set in imaginary worlds, but she also writes about the Pacific Northwest. *Searoad* is set on the Oregon coast, and *Blue Moon over Thurman Street* is set in Leguin's own Portland neighborhood.

Ken Kesey is another Oregon writer who uses the Pacific Northwest in his work. Kesey was born in Colorado. He was introduced to the Northwest when his family moved to Oregon. He went to high school in Springfield and later attended the University of Oregon in Eugene.

Kesey's most famous book is *One Flew over the Cuckoo's Nest*, which was published in 1962. It takes place in the mental ward of

Ken Kesey in 1966. Kesey worked as a logger to get background experience for Sometimes a Great Notion, *one of his best-known novels.*

a hospital. Kesey based parts of the book on his real-life experience as a hospital night worker. The book asks the question, "How do we know who is crazy and who is sane?"

One Flew over the Cuckoo's Nest is about people who struggle to remain true to themselves even when society pressures them to be like everyone else. Kesey values people who are different. He once said, "If people could just understand that it is possible to be different without being a threat."

Sometimes a Great Notion, Kesey's next book, is the story of the Stampers, a logging family on the Oregon coast. Kesey worked as a logger near the town of Florence to get background for the book. Both of his first two books were made into movies. His most recent book is *Sailor Song*, published in 1992. Kesey takes a long time over each new book. "I feel that I have an obligation to improve," he says, "and I worry about that."

Kids everywhere have read the books of Beverly Cleary, who was born in 1916 in McMinnville, south of Portland. She has written many children's books and won so many awards that it would take a whole page just to list them.

Cleary was hooked on books from an early age. Her mother started the town's first lending library. Cleary later recalled, "It was in this dingy room filled with shabby leather-covered chairs and smelling of stale cigar smoke that I made the most magical of discoveries. There were books for children!"

Cleary's family moved to Portland, and she looked forward to learning to read. But when she started reading, she was disappointed. Children's books all seemed to be about English children who rode ponies and were too polite. "I wanted to read funny stories about the sort of children I knew," Cleary said. "I decided that someday when I grew up I would write them."

Beverly Cleary did just that. Most of her stories take place around Klickitat Street—the street in northeast Portland where she lived when she was growing up. Her most beloved character is Ramona Quimby, who appears in many of her books. Ramona, said one

AN HONORED POET

Poet William Stafford (1914–1993) lived in Lake Oswego, just outside Portland. He won the National Book Award and many other awards, and the state of Oregon honored him as its official poet.

Many of Stafford's poems use images of animals, trees, and the natural world. This poem is from a book of Stafford's poems called *An Oregon Message*:

Starting with Little Things

Love the earth like a mole,
fur-near. Nearsighted,
their fine-print headlines.
Pat them with soft hands—

But spades, but pink and loving: they
break rock, nudge giants aside,
affable plow.
Fields are to touch:
each day nuzzle your way.

Tomorrow the world.

reader, is a "very real little girl trying to understand and be understood in a bewildering world."

THE ARTS

Ay, caramba! One of Oregon's most famous artists is Matt Groening, the creator of *The Simpsons*. Groening was born in Portland in 1954. He says he had "the hippest dad in the neighborhood. By

At Lincoln High School in Portland, Matt Groening scribbled drawings in his notebooks. Today he is famous as the creator of Bart Simpson and other cartoon characters.

example he showed that you could do whatever you wanted to in life."

Young Groening loved to draw. One Portlander who went to school with Groening at Lincoln High remembers that Groening's notebooks were always covered with doodles of "kids with spiky hair." Today Lincoln High has a sculpture of one of those spiky-haired kids: Bart Simpson.

Groening moved to Los Angeles and began publishing a comic strip. His big break came in 1990 when *The Simpsons*, an animated series using his characters, first appeared on television. Matt Groening used his parents' and his sisters' names for Homer, Marge, Lisa, and Maggie Simpson. He made up the name Bart, though—from the letters of *brat*.

The Simpsons won an Emmy Award for best animated series and has earned Groening a fortune. But, he says, "Most of all, I'm in this business to have fun. One of the greatest thrills of my life is that I now get paid for what I used to get sent to the principal's office for."

Music Scene. Grunge rock was born in the Pacific Northwest. Oregon has had its share of bands that have moved up from playing in garages to making best-selling albums. One of the best-known is Everclear, from Portland.

Portland's music scene is lively. Dozens of clubs feature talented local bands. Young people crowd the clubs, hoping to catch the nearest supergroup on the rise. Two of the region's biggest music events each year are the Waterfront Blues Festival in Portland and the Mount Hood Festival of Jazz in Gresham. Dozens of other music festivals take place around the state, from the annual Oregon

Everclear at the MTV Video Music Awards, 1996. The rock group is one of many Portland bands that have won national followings.

Bach Festival in Eugene to the Medford Jazz Jubilee in southern Oregon.

Classical music is alive and well in Oregon. James DePriest, music director of the Oregon Symphony, has been honored around the world for his contributions to symphonic music.

DePriest grew up in Philadelphia. As an African American, he overcame barriers of racial prejudice to become a classical conductor. A greater barrier, however, was polio, which struck him just as his career was beginning and left his legs paralyzed. Refusing to give up his dream, DePriest forced himself to stand firmly braced while conducting. Eventually he began conducting from his wheel-chair and found it "very freeing."

DePriest credits his childhood for setting him on the right path. He was raised in an ethnically mixed neighborhood by a houseful of strong women. "I had everything I needed and much of what I wanted. I had the sense that anything I wanted to accomplish I could if I was qualified."

James DePriest conducted in Europe in the 1960s, then in the United States and Canada before coming to Portland in 1980. One member of the Oregon Symphony said, "There are few orchestras in America that have the same affection for their maestro as we

Music director James DePriest took charge of the Oregon Symphony in 1980. Under his leadership, the orchestra has introduced programs such as outdoor concerts in Portland's neighborhood parks.

have for Jimmy. A lot of conductors forget that they're dealing with people. Jimmy never forgets that. As a result, we'd do just about anything for him."

Films. Movies are the most popular art form in the United States, and Oregon has been the setting for several hit films. Astoria, for example, is the setting for *Free Willy* and *Kindergarten Cop*, and parts of *The River Wild* were filmed along the Rogue River. Oregon also has its own star moviemaker.

Gus Van Sant was born in Kentucky, grew up in Connecticut, and

Filmmaker Gus Van Sant has used Portland as the setting of successful films starring young actors such as Matt Dillon and Keanu Reeves.

now lives in a large Victorian house in Portland's costly West Hills neighborhood. A movie critic writing for *Newsweek* magazine called Van Sant "the freshest new voice working in American movies."

Van Sant's fame rests on two movies he directed. Both are set in and around Portland. *Drugstore Cowboy*, starring Matt Dillon, explored the lives of young drug addicts in the 1970s. *My Own Private Idaho*, starring Keanu Reeves and River Phoenix, looked at the troubled lives of two Portland street kids. Although his movies look at the dark side of life, Van Sant thinks Portland is a pretty sunny place. "Everything's tame and sort of friendly," he says.

POLITICS AND SCIENCE

For thirty years Mark O. Hatfield represented Oregon in the U.S. Senate. Many Americans came to respect him for the way he always stood up for what he believed was right.

Hatfield was born in Dallas, Oregon, in 1922. He grew up in Salem, close to the center of state government. During World War II Hatfield served in the navy. He was at the battles of Iwo Jima and Okinawa in the Pacific, two of the most brutal conflicts of the war. He was also one of the first American servicemen to see what the Japanese city of Hiroshima was like after the United States dropped an atomic bomb on it to end the war. Hatfield's war experiences convinced him that it was better to work for peace than to seek war.

After returning to Oregon, Hatfield entered politics as a state senator in 1950. In 1956 he was elected governor. He was the youngest governor in the state's history. He was elected to the U.S.

For thirty years Mark O. Hatfield was a powerful voice in Washington, D.C., calling for peace and environmental protection.

Senate in 1966. The Vietnam War was raging during Hatfield's first years in the Senate. Most Republicans supported the war, but although Hatfield was a Republican, he never hesitated to say that he thought the war was wrong.

In 1980 Hatfield was made chairman of the Senate Appropriations Committee, one of the most powerful groups in Congress. He continued to support antiwar efforts, and he argued that the United States should spend less money on nuclear weapons and more on education.

Hatfield also became known as a politician who was open about his Christian beliefs. "I pray for the integrity, justice, and courage to vote the correct vote, not the political vote," he once said. "It's a reckless style of politics, but it's the only style I know." In 1996, after nearly half a century in politics, Mark Hatfield retired from the Senate.

Linus Pauling is probably the most famous scientist Oregon has

Dr. Linus Pauling in 1985, with close-ups of butterflies' wings arranged to spell out his name

produced. He was born in 1901 in Lake Oswego, south of Portland, the son of a pharmacist. The young Pauling was always drawn to science. As a child he collected insects and minerals, and as a teenager he carried out chemistry experiments.

Pauling did not graduate from high school—he refused to take a test because he had already shown that he knew the material. He managed to get admitted to Oregon Agricultural College (now Oregon State University) anyway. Later he went to other schools for advanced study in chemistry.

In 1954 Pauling won chemistry's highest honor, the Nobel Prize for chemistry. He was awarded the prize for research he had done into the shape of chemical compounds.

At about the same time, Pauling began his fight to stop the testing of nuclear weapons. In 1958 he published a book called *No More War!* He gave the U.S. Congress a petition, signed by eleven thousand scientists from forty-nine countries, that asked for an end to nuclear testing. Pauling refused to tell the Congress who had helped him gather the signatures. In a time when some people thought that working for peace was un-American, Pauling did not want anyone to get into trouble for helping him.

For his antiwar activism Pauling was rewarded with the Nobel Peace Prize in 1962. Then, after two Nobel prizes, his old high school finally granted him his diploma.

In his later years Pauling focused his research on vitamins, especially vitamin C. He believed that vitamin C could prevent colds and help people live longer. Although Pauling's ideas have found millions of believers around the world, scientists still debate the value of taking Vitamin C.

SPORTS

In Oregon the word *sports* usually means something that you do, not something that you watch. Oregon has only one big-league sports team, the Portland Trail Blazers of the National Basketball Association. But at games in the new Rose Garden Arena, Blazers fans get fired up with what they call Blazermania.

Two other teams play in Portland, although not in the big leagues. They are the Winterhawks hockey team and the Rockies baseball team. "Maybe they're not the biggest in the world," said a Rockies fan, "but it sure is fun to come to a game and cheer. This is real old-fashioned baseball, not big business."

Mary Decker Slaney, a runner, is perhaps Oregon's best-known individual athlete. She was born in Eugene in 1958 and entered her first race at eleven. She won. "Even if I hadn't won," she said later, "I would still have been captivated. After that, all I wanted to do was run."

In 1982 Mary Decker Slaney set a world record for the mile and 10,000-meter runs and an American record for the 3,000-meter run. She was the first woman to receive the Jesse Owens International Amateur Athletic Award, given yearly to the world's best track-and-field competitor. The next year she won two gold medals at the International Track and Field Championships in Finland.

Despite her successes, Mary Decker Slaney's career held one big disappointment: She never won an Olympic medal. She was a member of the U.S. team for several Olympic events, but injuries, bad luck, and bad timing kept her from performing at her best. In 1996 Mary Decker Slaney made one last attempt to capture an

"I've been lucky and I've been unlucky," says Mary Decker Slaney of her running career. "All I can say is that I've done my best."

Olympic medal. When she failed, she smiled and said with true Olympic spirit, "I wish I'd done better, but I just wanted to be here, and I had a great time."

6 OREGON
ROAD TRIP

"**O**regon is one of the coolest states we've seen," said Heather McDonald, who has toured twenty-three states in her family's camper. "I want to come back again so I can see everything here!"

Lots of people feel the same way. Oregonians like traveling around their state as much as visitors do. Any tour of Oregon should start with Portland, Oregon's largest city and center of cultural activities.

A CITY OF MANY NAMES

Portland has grown a lot since Asa Lovejoy and Francis Pettygrove flipped their coin to choose its name. Back then Portland was a small landing area on the west side of the Willamette River. But Portland soon began sprawling out in all directions. In the early days people called the city Stumptown because so many stumps were left standing where trees had been cut down to make room for roads and buildings.

Docks and warehouses were built along the river to handle the city's shipping trade. Portland is still a busy harbor town. Super-tankers and cruise ships come all the way up the Columbia and a few miles of the Willamette to dock there. The skyline along the river bristles with cargo cranes, and occasionally the great gray bulk of a navy ship looms above the dockside buildings.

Early Portlanders who grew wealthy built large homes on the

Portland's skyline is mirrored in the waters of the Willamette River. At right is the Hawthorne bridge, used every day by many of the city's bicycle commuters.

forested hills west of downtown. Immigrants and working-class people settled in neighborhoods north and south of downtown. Soon people were living and working on the east side of the Willamette, too.

At first the only way to go from one side of Portland to the other was by ferry. Then, in 1887, Portlanders built the first of many bridges across the river. The bridge's owners charged five cents each for people, sheep, and hogs to cross. Today ten bridges span the river in downtown Portland, which is sometimes called the City of Bridges. Anyone can cross them for free—but it has been a long time since a sheep or a hog tried to do so.

City of Roses is another of Portland's nicknames. Roses grow extremely well in the mild, moist climate of western Oregon, and the city is full of gardens that burst with their colors and scents. The International Rose Test Gardens, perched on a hill with a splendid view of Portland's skyline, is a flower lover's paradise with more than ten thousand rose bushes.

Roses are the theme of Portland's biggest annual event, the Rose Festival, which runs for nearly a month and includes dozens of activities, such as balloon rides, auto and boat races, and fireworks. The highlight of the festival is the Grand Floral Parade of floats decorated with flowers. It is the second-largest floral parade in the United States.

City of Fountains might be another good nickname for Portland. Downtown Portland is a mix of dazzling modern office towers—the tallest is the First Interstate Tower at forty-one stories—and small, inviting shops, coffee bars, and restaurants on almost every street. Scattered among the downtown blocks are half a dozen fountains, including one that was built to look like a mountain waterfall. On hot days kids play in all the fountains.

Two of Portland's most popular attractions are the zoo and the art museum. The Metropolitan Washington Park Zoo is Oregon's biggest paid attraction. It has arctic tundra and Pacific Northwest wildlife exhibits and much more. At Zoo Concerts, Portlanders picnic on a grassy lawn while folk, blues, and jazz musicians perform, and elephants sway to the music. The Portland Art

Young people cool off in a fountain outside the Rose Garden, the sports arena that is home to the Portland Trailblazers.

Museum, in the heart of downtown Portland, has collections of Native American, Asian, and African art as well as European and American paintings. More than forty-five thousand schoolchildren take part each year in the museum's programs for young people.

Kids also like the Oregon Museum of Science and Industry (OMSI) in southeast Portland. A real submarine, interactive science experiments, and a planetarium are just a few of its attractions.

History is the focus of many Oregon museums. In Portland the museum of the Oregon Historical Society features exhibits on all parts of Oregon's past. In nearby Oregon City, the End of the Oregon Trail Interpretive Center is a museum about the Oregon Trail. Every summer the center hosts a play called *Oregon Fever*, which captures the excitement of the settlers' journey west.

Portland is full of things to see and do—but so is the rest of the state. The Willamette Valley south of Portland has quiet back roads through gentle farm country. People now grow grapes and make wine in this part of Oregon, and winery tours are popular.

Visitors to Salem can tour the state capitol or stroll through neighborhoods where historic buildings have been preserved. One building, the home of missionary Jason Lee, was built in 1841. It is the oldest frame house in the Northwest.

A little to the west is the small town of Monmouth, home of the Paul Jensen Arctic Museum. It is the only arctic museum in the lower forty-eight states and has more than three thousand items related to the peoples of the arctic. Fifty thousand people have visited the museum since it opened in 1985.

THE COAST

Oregon has nearly four hundred miles of coastline—"the most beautiful in the world," insists a teenage girl from Florence. Pictures of Oregon's towering offshore rocks, misty capes, and curving beaches show up regularly on scenic calendars. One of the best things about the Oregon coast is that it belongs to everyone. In 1967 the state legislature passed the "beach bill," which opened all beaches to the public.

Astoria, at the north end of the coast, was the first permanent settlement in the American West. One of the town's modern attractions is the Columbia River Maritime Museum, a tribute to the region's seafaring history. Nearby is a replica of Fort Clatsop, where the Lewis and Clark expedition spent the winter of 1805–1806.

Lincoln City and Newport are two of the largest communities

The Salem residence of Jason Lee, the first Methodist missionary in Oregon. Lee also founded a school, which today is Salem's Willamette University.

At Cape Kiwanda, fishermen still put out to sea from the beach in small boats called dories.

on the central coast, full of shops and restaurants for the visitors who come there year-round. Along this stretch of coast are cliffs and capes where people gather to watch the majestic grey whales swim by on their yearly migrations. The whales swim south in December and January and north with their young in April and May.

Most of Oregon's coast is craggy and rocky. Between Florence

Southern Oregon's Boardman State Park is one of thirty-eight state parks on the coast.

and North Bend, however, is the forty-seven-mile-long Oregon Dunes National Recreation Area, a sweep of rolling white sand dunes. Farther south are Coos Bay, the largest city on the coast, and Bandon, which is the "storm-watching capital of Oregon" *and* the "cranberry capital of Oregon."

HEADING INLAND

Southern Oregon has something for everyone. Rafters and kayakers from all over the country come to the Rogue, one of the Wild and Scenic Waterways chosen by the U.S. Congress for protection from

Vacationing kids dig a sand cave in the Oregon Dunes National Recreation Area.

SAY HELLO TO KEIKO

One of the state's most popular attractions is the Oregon Coast Aquarium in Newport, which opened in 1992. There's no doubt who is the star of the aquarium: It's Keiko, the orca (sometimes called a killer whale) who starred in *Free Willy*. Visitors can watch Keiko in his large pool, but he is no longer a performing whale who does stunts for the public. Whale experts are working with Keiko, teaching him the skills he will need to know if he is ever released into the open sea. The goal of those who care for Keiko is to set him free someday.

dams and development. The Rogue and other rivers in the area also offer salmon and steelhead trout fishing.

Highway 199 leads south through Oregon's redwood country. It passes through the small town of Cave Junction, the gateway to the Oregon Caves National Monument. In 1874 Elijah Davidson and his dog Bruno were chasing a bear when Bruno seemed to vanish. The dog had discovered the entrance to one of the most spectacular cave systems in the United States. Four million people have toured the caves since President William H. Taft declared them a national monument in 1909. "Caveman weddings," with the barefoot bride and groom dressed in furs, used to be held deep in the caves.

The town of Ashland, nestled in the southern mountains, is the site of Oregon's most famous theater event: the annual Oregon Shakespeare Festival. Each year, from February through October, actors perform eleven plays in Ashland. Four of the plays are by Shakespeare. The festival has won many dramatic awards and brings thousands of visitors to southern Oregon.

Most of these visitors make time to visit Crater Lake National Park and see the deepest lake in the United States. For years people have tried to describe the dazzling dark blue color of the lake's water. A visitor in 1854 called it "the bluest water I ever saw." He thought the lake ought to be called Mysterious Lake or Deep Blue Lake. Poet Walt Curtis described the color this way: "Water mirrors blue sky . . . Lonesome blue planet earth."

Crossing the Cascades, the traveler enters central and eastern Oregon. Highway 395 from Lakeview to Burns passes through the "Oregon outback," a rugged region of mountains, deserts, and lake-

Seen from the air, Crater Lake is a sapphire set in a ring of silver-white hills. An 1854 visitor dubbed it Mysterious Lake.

side wetlands. Wildlife and fossils outnumber people in this part of the state.

Farther northeast are the Wallowa Mountains and Hells Canyon. A drive to the town of Joseph, named for the Nez Percé leader, heads into the heart of the mountains, where a monument to the chief stands on the shore of Wallowa Lake. Forest roads, closed in winter because of snow, run east to the rim of Hells Canyon and a mile-deep view.

WHAT KIND OF NAME IS THAT?

Weird names are sprinkled across the map of Oregon. Take Helix, a tiny town in the northeast. Legend says it was named by an early resident who had an earache. His doctor told him that a part of his ear called the helix was infected. He liked the name and used it for the town.

How would you like to live in a town called Boring? "This is really *not* a dull place!" one citizen of Boring insisted, explaining that the town was named after old-time resident W. H. Boring. But Remote, a tiny community near the coast, got its name because it is far away from other settlements.

Donner und Blitzen Creek, which flows into Malheur Lake, was not named for two of Santa's tiny reindeer. In 1864 army troops crossed the creek in a thunderstorm and gave it the German name for "thunder and lightning."

Many Oregon place-names are Indian words. *Yakso* is a Chinook word meaning "hair," and the seventy-foot Yakso Falls on the Little River resemble a woman's long, flowing hair. Central Oregon has a town, a lake, a mountain, and a creek named Paulina, but they weren't named for some lonely settler's sweetheart. Paulina, or Paunina, was a chieftain of the Snake Indians who fought settlers in the 1860s.

You can find more place-names and the stories behind them in a book called *Oregon Geographic Names*.

Between the Wallowas and the Columbia River is Pendleton. This part of Oregon is filled with museums and historic markers, reminders of the days when the Oregon Trail passed through. It is also sheep country, and Pendleton is a wool-processing center. The world-famous Pendleton wool blankets, usually decorated with

PLACES TO SEE

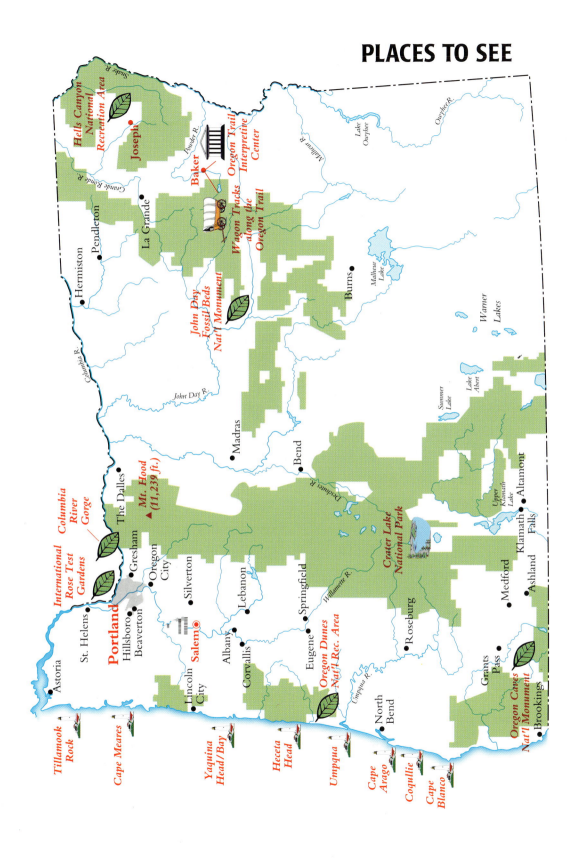

Hells Canyon National Recreation Area

Snake R.

Joseph

Powder R.

Oregon Trail Interpretive Center

Baker

Wagon Tracks along the Oregon Trail

Grande Ronde R.

La Grande

Pendleton

Hermiston

Columbia R.

Malheur R.

Lake Ouyhee

Ouyhee R.

Burns

Malheur Lake

Warner Lakes

John Day Fossil Beds Nat'l Monument

John Day R.

Summer Lake

Lake Abert

Madras

Bend

Deschutes R.

Mt. Hood ▲ (11,239 ft.)

The Dalles

Columbia River Gorge

International Rose Test Gardens

Gresham

Oregon City

Silverton

Lebanon

Springfield

Crater Lake National Park

Upper Klamath Lake

Altamont

Klamath Falls

Portland

Hillsboro
Beaverton

Salem

Albany

Corvallis

Eugene

Willamette R.

Roseburg

Medford

Ashland

St. Helens

Grants Pass

Oregon Dunes Nat'l Rec. Area

Umpqua R.

Lincoln City

Astoria

North Bend

Oregon Caves Nat'l Monument

Brookings

Tillamook Rock

Cape Meares

Yaquina Head/Bay

Heceta Head

Umpqua

Cape Arago

Coquille

Cape Blanco

Western or Indian designs, are made here. Pendleton is also the site of one of the biggest rodeos in the United States, the Pendleton Round-Up, a weeklong event every September.

Central Oregon offers a window into the distant past. In the nineteenth century scientists began finding fossils by the thousands along the John Day River. Today the John Day Fossil Beds National Monument protects three fossil fields. Visitors are welcome to tour them, but don't expect to see dinosaur bones. The fossils found here are relics of plants, turtles, rhinos, bear-dogs, pigs, and horses that lived from 45 to 5 million years ago.

Bend is central Oregon's biggest city. Outdoor recreation has grown into one of the region's most important businesses, and Bend and the nearby town of Redmond have grown along with it. These sell supplies and services to people who want to ski at Mount Bachelor, raft or kayak the Deschutes River white water, or hike and camp in the Deschutes and Ochoco National Forests.

Rock climbers from all over the world test their skill at nearby Smith Rock State Park, where spires and cliffs rise sheer above the canyon of the Crooked River. People who don't climb like Smith Rock, too. They can stroll comfortable pathways and watch the climbers creep like brightly colored spiders up the red rock walls.

Several hours' drive north of Bend the Columbia River flows through the majestic Gorge, a National Scenic Area. "I've seen just about every part of Oregon," says Portlander Jim Schull, "and the Gorge is still my favorite." The wide river winds between hills and cliffs that change from sunbaked golden brown in the east to mossy green in the west. There are more than a dozen waterfalls on Oregon's side of the Gorge. Multnomah Falls is the state's highest

In the John Day Fossil Beds thousands of fossil finds have opened a window into the earth's past.

The most popular sight in the Columbia Gorge. "If there's anything more beautiful than Multnomah Falls," Gresham resident Carla Macomber says, "I want to hear about it."

at 620 feet. A narrow scenic highway takes visitors over arched bridges and through tunnels up to Crown Point, a lookout on one of the highest spots in the Gorge. To the southeast Mount Hood rears its pointed crown. To the southwest lies Portland, where our journey began.

Oregonians can't decide whether to show off their state or keep it to themselves. They are proud of Oregon, and they welcome the money that tourists bring to the state. At the same time, they are afraid that too many people will move to Oregon and "ruin" it. Tom McCall, a former governor of Oregon, used to say, "Visit our state of enchantment—but for heaven's sakes, don't stay!"

In 1980 McCall said that Oregon was becoming more crowded and that Oregonians were complaining that the future didn't look as bright as it used to. Then he added that if Oregonians make the right decisions, "we can still live on in a way that will let us boast, 'You bet, the future is what it used to be.'"

THE FLAG: *The flag was adopted in 1925. It displays a special version of the gold state seal on a navy blue background. On the flag, the words "State of Oregon" and the date "1859" from the state seal have been enlarged.*

THE SEAL: *The state seal was adopted in 1859, the year Oregon became a state. Just inside the sealborder are 33 stars representing Oregon as the thirty-third state. The stars enclose a shield topped by the Federal eagle. The British ship leaving and an American ship arriving show that Oregon was never controlled by a foreign government. The ox-drawn wagon beneath the ships stands for the settlement of Oregon by means of the Oregon Trail. The trees, grain, farmer's plow, and miner's pick represent the state's natural resources and industries.*

STATE SURVEY

Statehood: February 14, 1859

Origin of Name: Uncertain, but probably named for the Columbia River. The river was once called the Oregon, or *Ouragan*, French for "hurricane."

Nickname: The Beaver State

Capital: Salem

Motto: She Flies With Her Own Wings

Bird: Western meadowlark

Animal: Beaver

Flower: Oregon grape

Tree: Douglas fir

Insect: Oregon swallowtail

Nut: Hazelnut

Fish: Chinook salmon

Rock: Thunderegg

Gemstone: Sunstone

Colors: Navy blue and gold

Dance: Square dance

Western meadowlark

Oregon grape

OREGON, MY OREGON

Judge John A. Buchanan's poem "Oregon, My Oregon" was set to music by three different composers in a 1920 competition for official state song. This winning composition was adopted by the state legislature in 1927.

Words by John A. Buchanan   **Music by Henry B. Murtagh**

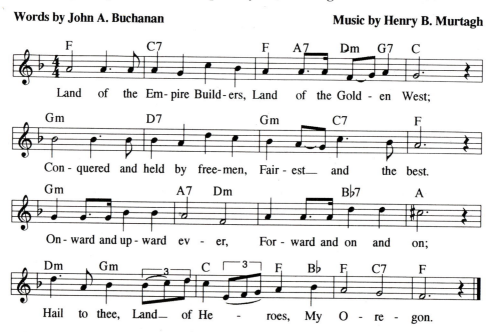

GEOGRAPHY

Highest Point: 11,235 feet above sea level, at Mt. Hood

Lowest Point: sea level, along the Pacific coast

Area: 98,386 square miles

Greatest Distance North to South: 295 miles

Greatest Distance East to West: 395 miles

Bordering States: Washington to the north, Idaho to the east, Nevada to the southeast and east, California to the south

Hottest Recorded Temperature: 119°F at Prineville on July 29, 1896, and at Pendleton on August 10, 1898

Coldest Recorded Temperature: −54°F at Ukiah on February 9, 1933, and at Seneca on February 10, 1933

Average Annual Precipitation: 28 inches

Major Rivers: Columbia, Deschutes, John Day, Owyhee, Rogue, Snake, Umpqua, Willamette

Major Lakes: Abert, Blue River, Bluejoint, Campbell, Chinook, Crane Prairie, Crater, Detroit, Fern Ridge, Flagstaff, Foster, Harney, Hart, Lookout Point, Malheur, Prineville, Summer, Upper Klamath, Waldo, Wallowa

Trees: alder, ash, cottonwood, Douglas fir, Engelmann spruce, juniper, lodgepole pine, madrone, maple, ponderosa pine, sugar pine, western hemlock, western red cedar, western white pine, willow

Wild Plants: buckbrush, bunch grass, camas lily, Indian paintbrush, juniper, Oregon grape, red huckleberry, sagebrush

Animals: antelope, beaver, bighorn sheep, bobcat, coyote, deer, elk, fox, mink, mountain goat, muskrat, river otter, sea lion, sea otter, seal, whale

Birds: bald eagle, duck, goose, grebe, grouse, hawk, heron, osprey, pelican, sandpiper, sora, spotted owl, swan, warbler, woodpecker

Fish: perch, salmon, steelhead trout, striped bass, sturgeon

Endangered Animals: black right whale, blue whale, fin whale, grey whale, grey wolf, humpback whale, sei whale, sperm whale

Sperm whale

Endangered Plants: Applegates's milk vetch, big-flowered wooly meadow-foam, Bradshaw's desert-parsley, Cook's desert-parsley, crinite mariposa lily, Cusick's lupine, Dalles Mountain buttercup, Gentner's fritillary, golden paintbrush, Grimy ivesia, Howell's thelypody, MacFarlane's four-o'clock, Malheur wire-lettuce, Mulford's milk vetch, northern wormwood, Owyhee clover, pink sand verbena, red-fruited lomatium, rough allocarya, saltmarsh bird's-beak, shiny-fruited allocarya, smooth mentzelia, Snake River goldenweed, Spalding's campion, Umpqua mariposa lily, western lily, white rock larkspur, Willamette daisy

TIMELINE

Oregon History

c. 8000 B.C. Native Americans enter the region that will become Oregon

1579 Sir Francis Drake may have landed on the Oregon coast

1778 James Cook sails along the Oregon coast and names Cape Foul-weather

1792 Captain Robert Gray sails into the Columbia River and names it for his ship

1805 Lewis and Clark reach the Pacific Ocean at the mouth of the Columbia River

1811 John Jacob Astor founds Astoria as a fur-trading post

1819 Spain surrenders its land claim north of 42° north latitude, establishing Oregon's straight southern border at this line

1824 John McLoughlin, the "father of Oregon," becomes the director of the Hudson's Bay Company in Oregon

1834 The first permanent settlement in the Willamette Valley is founded by missionaries

1841 Settlers begin moving west on the Oregon Trail

1843 The first large group of immigrants traveling the Oregon Trail arrive in the Willamette Valley

1848 Oregon becomes a territory

1850 Congress passes the Oregon Donation Land Law, which gives land to settlers in the Oregon Territory

1850 The territorial government is moved to Salem

1851 Oregon's first public school opens

1853 Congress creates Washington Territory, which establishes Oregon's present boundaries

1859 Oregon becomes a state

1872–1873 U.S. troops battle the Modoc Indians in the Modoc Wars

1877 U.S. troops battle the Nez Percé in the Nez Percé War

1912 Women are granted the right to vote in Oregon

1937 The Bonneville Dam is completed, making the Columbia River navigable

1940 The population of Oregon passes one million

1950 Oregon becomes the nation's leading lumber state

1964 Floods in western Oregon cause widespread damage

1985 Oregon adopts a state lottery

ECONOMY

Agricultural Products: beans, beef cattle, berries, cherries, chickens, clover, corn, dairy cattle, flower bulbs, grass seed, hay, hazelnuts, hogs, hops, onions, pears, peas, plums, potatoes, sheep, sugar beets, timber (Douglas fir and ponderosa pine), wheat

Manufactured Products: computers, electrical equipment, frozen fruits and vegetables, lumber, machinery, paper, paperboard, particleboard, plywood, scientific instruments, veneer

Natural Resources: clays, copper, diatomite, gold, gravel, lead, limestone, natural gas, nickel, pumice, sand, silver chromium, soils, stone, timber, water

Business and Trade: finance, insurance, international trade, printing and publishing, real estate, tourism

CALENDAR OF CELEBRATIONS

Portland Cinco de Mayo Cinco de Mayo is held on May 5 to celebrate the anniversary of Mexico's defeat of a French army in 1867. In Portland, the city's Mexican-American population hosts a huge, happy celebration that is one of the largest Hispanic celebrations in the Pacific Northwest.

Oregon Shakespeare Festival The plays of William Shakespeare and others come to life every year in Ashland from February through October.

Portland Rose Festival Oregon is famous for its flowers. The rose takes center stage every June in Portland. Carnivals, concerts, and other events add to the festive atmosphere, which is capped off by the Grand Floral Parade.

Grand Floral Parade, Portland Rose Festival

Cannon Beach Sand Castle Contest Contestants try to outdo each other by building the largest and fanciest sand castles they can each June. More than 100 sand castles dot the beach until the tide washes them away.

Da Vinci Days Science and technology are celebrated at this unique science festival held every July in Corvallis. There are many displays and hands-on exhibits in this festival, which is named for Leonardo da Vinci.

July 4th Parade Each Independence Day, Hillsboro hosts the largest patriotic parade in the state.

World Championship Timber Carnival Oregon leads the country in timber production, and loggers and lumberjacks participate in such contests as log-rolling each Independence Day weekend in Albany.

Oregon Bach Festival Each summer, baroque music is celebrated through several performances at the beautiful Hult Center in Eugene.

Oregon Country Fair This summertime fair, held in July in Elmira, is the place to see some of the finest arts and crafts the state has to offer.

Oregon State Fair Horse races, a rodeo, and great food are some of the main attractions at "Oregon's biggest show," held each August in Salem.

Fall International Kite Festival The beautiful countryside around Lincoln City becomes even more colorful during this September celebration. Thousands of kites fill the sky.

Pendleton Round-Up and Happy Canyon Pageant Oregon's western heritage is celebrated during this rodeo. Musical shows and dances round out the September celebration.

Festival of Lights at the Grotto The holiday season is brightened each

December with a beautiful display of Christmas lights in the trees at Portland's famous gardens.

STATE STARS

James Beard (1903–1985) was the nation's leading authority on food and cooking for more than 50 years. Born in Portland, he wrote more than 20 books on "good cooking," and was a pioneer in sophisticated outdoor cuisine.

Ernest Bloch

Ernest Bloch (1880–1959) was a composer whose name is familiar to every concert violinist. His music drew from the Jewish tradition. Bloch studied and taught in Europe and America. He retired to Agate Beach, where he composed music and enjoyed the Oregon coast.

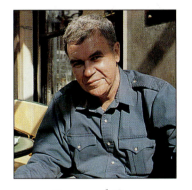

Raymond Carver

Raymond Carver (1938 –1988) is celebrated for his poems and short stories that depict the lives of the working poor. Carver was born in Clatskanie. His Oregon heritage can be seen in his poetry collection *Near Klamath* and in his other works.

Abigail Scott Duniway (1834–1915) was a leader of the women's suffrage movement in the northwest. After moving to Oregon as a teenager, she later founded the Oregon Equal Suffrage Association. When Oregon women were granted the right to vote, Duniway was hailed for her work.

Dick Fosbury

Dick Fosbury (1947–   ) was born in Medford and attended Oregon State University. There he invented a new approach to the high jump. He flipped over the bar backward in a move that became known as the "Fosbury Flop." He set an Olympic record in the 1948 summer Olympic Games in Mexico City. High jumpers around the world now use the jump Fosbury invented.

John E. Frohnmeyer (1942–   ), who was appointed chairman of the National Endowment of the Arts in 1989, is a long-time supporter of the arts. Born in Medford, he has helped choose public artworks for the city of Eugene and for the Capitol in Salem. He served as chairman of the Oregon Arts Commission prior to 1989.

Matt Groening (1954–   ) is the creator of *The Simpsons* television show. Born in Portland, his love of cartooning started when he was in elementary school. The success of *The Simpsons* has led to the creation of more than 200 products. Despite his success, Groening says, "Most of all, I'm in this business to have fun."

Mark Hatfield (1922–   ) served in the United States Senate from 1966 to 1996. He was born in Dallas, Oregon, and was elected to the state legislature in 1950. He served as a representative for four years and then as a state senator for two more years. After serving as Oregon's Secretary of state, he was elected governor in 1959.

Donald P. Hodel (1935–   ) was born in Portland. He served as the secretary of energy and later the secretary of the interior under President Reagan. He was controversial because he favored opening public lands to oil companies and supported the development of nuclear power.

Dave Kingman (1948–   ) is a heavy-hitting baseball player known as Dave "Kong" Kingman. Born in Pendleton, he broke Little League records as a young ballplayer. This right-hander, a reliable long-distance hitter (he has several three-homer games to his credit) has played for many teams.

Dave Kingman

Ursula K. LeGuin (1929–   ), is among the greatest science fiction and fantasy writers and one of Portland's leading residents. She began writing at age nine. Her novels address many issues in fantastic settings.

Edwin Markham (1852–1940), a great poet, was born in a log cabin in Oregon City. From these simple beginnings, he rose to become the "Dean of American Poetry." Markham's most famous works are "The Man with the Hoe" and *Lincoln, Man of the People.* Today, a century-and-a-half after his birth, his poems are still widely read and admired.

Edwin Markham

Tom McCall (1913–1983) grew up on the family ranch near Prineville. As a boy he loved Oregon's great outdoors. As governor from 1967 to 1975, he fought hard to preserve Oregon's natural beauty and resources.

Joaquin Miller (1837–1913) traveled from Indiana to Oregon as a boy. He became a showman and poet, relating exciting tales about life in Oregon and other parts of the American West. His autobiography tells the tale of his life among the Modoc Indians.

Linus Pauling (1901–1994) was born in Portland. A brilliant chemist, he received the Nobel Prize in Chemistry in 1954. Pauling worked to ban nuclear weapons tests. He spearheaded an antitesting petition drive, which more than 11,000 scientists from around the world signed. The petition urged the United Nations to work to stop nuclear testing and helped lead to a Nuclear Test Ban Treaty in 1963. Pauling was awarded the Nobel Peace Prize in 1962. Pauling also championed the use of vitamin C as an important part of a healthy diet.

John Reed (1887–1920) was born into a wealthy Oregon family in Portland. As a young journalist, he covered the Mexican Revolution and World War I. As his interest in social problems grew, he moved to Russia and became a supporter of the Bolsheviks. He died in Russia and was buried in the Kremlin. His book *Ten Days That Shook the World* is an eyewitness account of the Russian Revolution.

John Reed

Alberto Salazar (1958–   ) is one of the greatest long-distance runners of all time. As a student at the University of Oregon, he qualified for the U.S. Olympic team. Salazar won the New York Marathon three years in a row and was also victorious in the Boston Marathon.

William E. Stafford (1914–1990) was a leading American poet. He won the prestigious National Book Award in 1963 for his book of verse *Traveling through the Dark*. In 1975 he was named the Poet Laureate of Oregon, a post he held until his death.

Alberto Salazar

TOUR THE STATE

Dee Wright Observatory (Sisters) This is the site of Oregon's largest lava flow. A trail lets visitors explore the bizarre landscape—where astronauts trained before heading to the moon.

Newberry National Volcanic Monument (LaPine) The world's largest obsidian flow, odd lava formations, and beautiful waterfalls and lakes are discussed by National Forest Service naturalists, who conduct walking tours of this one-of-a-kind place.

Smith Rock State Park (Redmond) One of the most beautiful places in

Smith Rock State Park

a beautiful state, this park offers stunning views of spectacular rock formations.

Malheur National Wildlife Refuge (Burns) More than 250 species of birds—including trumpeter swans—thrive in this refuge. Many mammals, such as antelope and mink, can also be seen here.

Hells Canyon National Recreation Area (Joseph) At the overlook, visitors stand more than a mile above the floor of the deepest gorge in North America.

National Historic Oregon Trail Interpretive Center (Baker City) Visitors learn about the hardships and joys of life on the Oregon Trail by viewing the many exhibits and reenactments here.

John Day Fossil Beds National Monument (John Day) More than 50 million years of earth's history are visible in this rich landscape. Saber-toothed tigers and giant pigs once roamed here, and their fossils are on display.

Collier State Park (Klamath Falls) Explore Oregon's most important industry at the largest logging museum in the United States. Exhibits teach about the history and workings of the timber industry.

Crater Lake National Park Crater Lake is the deepest lake in the country and one of the most beautiful sites in the world. National park rangers explain the origin of the lake and point out the many plants and animals that thrive here.

Fort Clatsop National Memorial (Fort Clatsop) The fort Lewis and Clark built to survive the winter of 1805–1806 has been recreated. Guides discuss the fort and the many artifacts on display.

Oregon Coast Aquarium (Newport) An orca whale is a major attraction of this huge aquarium. Many other types of marine and coastal life can also be viewed here.

Oregon Dunes National Recreation Center (Florence) This "natural sandbox" is 47 miles long! Oregonians and tourists hike and camp along these beautiful sandy beaches year-round.

The Capitol (Salem) Daily tours teach about the history of Oregon and its beautiful capitol.

Gilbert House Children's Museum (Salem) This fun museum for children offers dozens of hands-on displays in 14 activity rooms. The museum focuses on arts, humanities, and the sciences. Activities range from making puppets to operating a model hydroelectric dam.

Corvallis Arts Center (Corvallis) Housed in a 100-year-old church, artworks are displayed year-round.

Portland Art Museum (Portland) The feature attraction of this museum is its Northwest Coast Indian collection, which is one of the most impressive of its kind.

The Willamette Science and Technology Center (Eugene) Young people of Eugene and visitors from all over participate in hands-on science and technology experiments and activities at "WISTEC."

University of Oregon Museum of Art (Eugene) This museum houses the Warner Collection of Oriental Art. This collection is among best-known collections of Asian artwork in the United States.

Oregon Museum of Science and Industry (Portland) A submarine and a planetarium are just two of the fascinating exhibits at the premier education facility in the Northwest.

Metro Washington Park Zoo (Portland) Instead of living in cages, the animals in this zoo thrive in specially-constructed natural habitats.

The Columbia River Gorge National Scenic Area The Columbia River Gorge is celebrated for its stunning natural beauty. Enjoy the view by hiking and camping along its banks, or travel through the gorge in a tour boat.

Bonneville Dam (Bonneville) This huge dam provides electric power and flood control along the Columbia River. Special "fish ladders" let salmon swimming upstream leap past the dam.

Mount Hood At 11,235 feet, this beautiful landmark is the highest mountain in the state. Dozens of campgrounds, hiking trails, and parks in the region offer breathtaking views of Mount Hood.

FUN FACTS

Portland is home to the world's smallest official park. Measuring just two feet across, Mill Ends Park was established as an official city park in 1976. It was created in 1948 as a home for leprechauns and a place to hold snail races on St. Patrick's Day.

The world's largest cheese factory, the Tillamook Cheese Factory, is located in Oregon.

FIND OUT MORE

If you'd like to find out more about Oregon, look in your school library, local library, bookstore, or video store. Here are some titles to ask for:

GENERAL STATE BOOKS

Bratvold, Gretchen. *Oregon.* Minneapolis: Lerner, 1991.

Fradin, Dennis. *Oregon.* Chicago: Childrens Press, 1995.

O'Donnell, Terence. *That Balance So Rare: The Story of Oregon.* Portland: Oregon Historical Society Press, 1988.

Stein, R. C. *America the Beautiful: Oregon.* Chicago: Childrens Press, 1989.

BOOKS ABOUT OREGON PEOPLE, PLACES, OR HISTORY

Friedman, Elaine S. *The Facts of Life in Portland.* Portland: Portland Possibilities, 1993.

O'Donnell, Terence, and Thomas Vaughan. *Portland: An Informal History and Guide.* Portland: Oregon Historical Society Press, 1984.

Smith, Katlin. *Portland Rainy Day Guide.* San Francisco: Chronicle Books, 1983.

Stefoff, Rebecca. *Children of the Westward Trail.* Brookfield, Connecticut: Millbrook Press, 1996.

Stefoff, Rebecca. *Lewis and Clark.* New York: Chelsea House, 1992.

Stein, R. C. *The Story of the Oregon Trail.* Chicago: Childrens Press, 1984.

VIDEOTAPES

The Columbia River Gorge: Chasm of Majesty. Encounter Video.

Gorgeous! Exploring the Columbia River Gorge. Portland: EMA Video Productions.

In Search of the Oregon Trail, 2 videocassettes. Lincoln: Nebraska ETV Network, 1996.

Step One to Portland and Vicinity. Seattle: Fisher Broadcasting, Inc., 1995.

CD-ROMS

Oregon Facts and Factivities. Decatur, Georgia: Gallopade Publishing, 1996. Carole Marsh Family CD-ROM.

The Oregon Trail. Minneapolis: MECC, 1993.

WEBSITES

Oregon Visitors Bureaus http://www.webcube.com/visitor/states/ore.htm

Oregon Home Page http://www.state.or.us/gov

INDEX

Page numbers for illustrations are in boldface.

Abernethy, George, 44
actors, **97**, 98
African Americans, 75, 76,
    76, 78, 95
agriculture, 20, **23**, 47, 60,
    61, 64, **64**, 66, 67, 130
Albany, 83
animals, 24
    endangered, 24, 128
    fossils, 120, **121**, 138
antiwar activism, 99, 101
aquarium, 115, 139
artists, 93-94
Ashland, 116
Asians, 75
Astoria, 111

Bandon, 114
beaches, 111, 114, **114**,
    132, 139
Beaverton, 83
Bend, 120
Bierstadt, Albert, "Mount
    Hood," **32**
birds, 24, **25**, 26
    spotted owl, 26
Boardman State Park, **112**
Boring, 118
bridges, **107**, 107-108
Broughton, William, 12
Brown, Tabitha, 42, **42**
business and industry, 61,
    62, 64, 66, 67, 131

camping, **82**
Cannady, Beatrice Morrow,
    76, **76**
canyons and gorges, 15, **16**,
    117, 120, 123, 138
Cape Kiwanda, 112
cartoon characters, 93-94
Cascade Range, 13, 17, **21**,
    22

Cave Junction, 116
caves, 116
celebrations, 59, **59**, **77**,
    79, **86**, 94-95, 108,
    116, 131-133
children's literature, 89, 91-
    93
Chinese, 72-73
Clark, William, 37, 38,
    111, 139
Cleary, Beverly, 91-93
climate, 17, 19-24, 127
    rain, 17, 19, **19**, 22
Coast Range, 20-21
Columbia River, 15, 16, 27,
    28-29, 30, 36, 37, 81,
    120, 127
Coos Bay, 114
Corvallis, 78, **80**, 81, 83,
    139
Crater Lake, **14**, 15, 116,
    117, 139
crime
    gangs, 75
    racism, 78-79
Curtis, Walt, 116

dams, 27, **30**
    song, 28-29
Davidson, Elijah, 116
DePriest, James, 95-97, **96**
Donner und Blitzen Creek,
    118

earthquakes, 15
economy, 27, 47-48, 58,
    60-62, 64, 66-67, 68,
    130-131
education
    cuts, 58, 80
    higher, 80-81
environmental protection,
    26, 30-31, 67, 69

ethnic groups, 9, 72-79
Eugene, 80, 83

fairs and festivals. *see* cele-
    brations
films. *see* motion pictures
fish, 24, **25**, 28, 30, 36, **84**,
    116
floods, 17
food recipe, 65, 79
forests, 20, **20**, 21, 22, 26,
    48, 61, 62, 81
fossils, 120, 138
fountains, 108, **109**

gardens, 108
German Americans, 79
ghost town, 85
gold mining, 47, 67
government
    branches, 54-56
    lawmaking reforms, 56-58
    Measure 5, 58
Granite, 85
Gray, Robert, 37
Gresham, 83, 94
Grey, Zane, 24
Groening, Matt, **93**, 93-94,
    134
Guthrie, Woody, 28

Hatfield, Mark, 98-100, **99**,
    134-135
health care, 81
Helix, 118
Hells Canyon, 15, 117, 138
Hillsboro, 83
Hispanics, 75, 77, 79
historic preservation, 9,
    110, **111**
history, 128-130
    exploration, 37-38
    Indian wars, 44, 45, **45**

Oregon Trail, 39-41, 42, **86**, 110, 118, 138
statehood, 44, 125
hydroelectric power, 27, 69, **69**

Jacksonville, 9
Japanese, 73, 74, **74**, 75, **77**
jobs, 48, 60, 61, 62, 75
John Day River, 120
Joseph, Chief, 45, 46, **46**, 117

Kesey, Ken, **90**, 90-91

lakes, **14**, 15, 23, 116, **117**, 127, 139
Lane, Joseph, 43, **43**
Lee, Jason, home, 110, **111**
LeGuin, Ursula K., 88-90, **89**, 135
Lewis, Meriwether, 38, 111, 139
Lincoln City, 111
Lovejoy, Asa, 43, 106

Malheur Lake, 23, 118
maps
    earning a living, 60
    land and water, 18
    places to see, 119
    road, 2
McCall, Tom, 123, 136
McLoughlin, John, 39
Medford, 83
Meek, Joe, 43
Meier, Julius, 48
Monmouth, 110
motion pictures, 91, **97**, 97-98
mountains, **10**, 13, **13**, 20-21, **21**, 22, 24, 126
Mount Hood, **10**, 13, **19**, 22, **32**, 126
Multnomah Falls, **122**, 123
museums, 108, 109, 110, 111, 139
music, 94-97, **95**, 108, 132

names, origin of, 118
Native Americans, 34, **35**,
36, 38, **39**, 44-46, **45**, **46**, 72, 79, 84, **84**, 88, 118
natural resources, 67, 69, 131
Newell, Robert, 54
Newport, 111, 115
Nobel Prize, 101

Oneonta Gorge, **16**
Oregon Dunes National Recreation Area, 114, **114**, 139

Painted Hills, **13**
parks, **112**, 120, 138, 139
Paulina, 118
Pauling, Linus, **100**, 100-101, 136
Pendleton, 118, 120
people, famous, 88-103, 133-137
Pettygrove, Francis, 43, 106
pioneers, 8, 16, 19, 27, 39-41, 54
plants, wild, 22, 127
poetry, 92
politicians, 98-100, **99**, 134-135
pollution, 30, 67
population, 9, 27, 38, 46, 47, 50, 51, 72, 83
Portland, 13, 15, 17, 27, 31, 44, 46, 48, 50, 79, 81, 83, 88, 94, 96, 97, 98, 102, 106-110, **107**, **109**
property tax, 58

racism, 78-79, **80**
ranching, **23**, 30-31, 47, 66, **66**
Redmond, 120
Reedsport, 62
religion, 77-78
Remote, 118
rivers, 15-16, 17, 24, 27, 127
rodeo, 120, 132
Rogue River, 114, 116
Russians, **73**

Sacajawea, 38, **39**
Salem, 44, **52**, 56, 59, **59**, 83, 110, 125
scientists, **100**, 100-101, 136
shipbuilding, 48, **50**
Slaney, Mary Decker, 102-103, **103**
Smith Rock State Park, 120, 138
Snake River, 15
songs
    dams, 28-29
    state, 126
sports, 81-82, 102-103, 120
    rock climbing, 120
    white water rafting, 15, 67, 114, 120
    windsurfing, **68**, 81
Springfield, 83
Stafford, William, 92, 137
Steens Mountain, 24
storytelling, 24, 27, 36, 88

theater, 116, 131
Tillamook, 72
timber, 47, 48, **49**, **50**, 61, 62, **63**, 64, 132, 139
Tisdale, Sallie, 8, 21
touring, 61, 67, 106-123, 137-139
trees, 20, **20**, 21, 22, 26, **49**, 127

Van Sant, Gus, 97-98
volcanoes, 13, 137

Wallowa Mountains, 22, 117
waterfalls, 120, 123
whale watching, 112, **115**
Wilhelm, Kate, 51
Willamette River, 16, 17, 106, **107**
winery, 110
writers, 88-93

Yakso Falls, 118

zoo, 108